HELP! MY PLANET IS MELTING!

HERE COMES GLOBAL WARMING!

By John Adlersparre

Note for Librarians: A cataloguing record for this book is available from
Library and Archives Canada at www.collectionscanada.ca/amicus/index-e.html
ISBN 1-4251-0364-2

TRAFFORD
PUBLISHING™

Offices in Canada, USA, Ireland and UK

Book sales for North America and international:
Trafford Publishing, 6E–2333 Government St.,
Victoria, BC V8T 4P4 CANADA
phone 250 383 6864 (toll-free 1 888 232 4444)
fax 250 383 6804; email to orders@trafford.com
Book sales in Europe:
Trafford Publishing (UK) Limited, 9 Park End Street, 2nd Floor
Oxford, UK OX1 1HH UNITED KINGDOM
phone 44 (0)1865 722 113 (local rate 0845 230 9601)
facsimile 44 (0)1865 722 868; info.uk@trafford.com
Order online at:
trafford.com/06-2121

10 9 8 7 6 5 4 3 2 1

Contents

Acknowledgements

The author wishes to thank the following people for their contribution to this book.

Wenche Adlersparre - Editor, contributor and critic. Each and every part of the book contains some of her artistic touch.

Ray Van Raamsdonk - Scientist and computer systems specialist. Ray dreamed up many ideas to express his thoughts about global warming.

Adrian Raeside - Incredible cartoon artist. His OTHER COAST comic strip appears in over 150 newspapers worldwide. Visit Adrian's web site at **http://www.raesidecartoon.com**

Jason Walton - Artist and animator. Designed the cover and other art pieces in the book. Jason's work can be seen at **http://members.shaw.ca/jasonwalton/**

INTRODUCTION

When my wife and I first heard about global warming heating up the earth, it was only natural for us to take contrary sides, as any couple would.

After numerous arguments and discussions, we decided the best approach would be to do our own research.

I wanted to go to the Arctic and measure the temperature in the glaciers, but only in the summer when it's warmer. She wanted to convince NASA to launch a million mirrors into space to reflect the sunlight away from earth.

I wanted to put a filter mask on everyone to measure how much carbon dioxide they produce. She wanted to get a research grant to study the effect of cruise ships on the climate, especially in Hawaii and the tropics.

But all those ideas were just too complicated so we compromised and collaborated on this book instead.

We thought the best approach would be to use words and pictures to explain what we believe everyone else is doing about global warming. We read publications, researched the Internet and eavesdropped whenever we could.

This is what we found.

John Adlersparre

COME ONE COME ALL
TO THE AMAZING
GLOBAL WARMING
CIRCUS

watch political clowns hide things in their disappearing budget bags!

watch Kyoto the magical clown make all the Global Warming disappear!

global warming

global cooling

green house gas

KYOTO

see the Lords of the Clown dance and catch as much research money as they can in their buckets!

watch the amazing juggling clowns throw facts in the air and catch them any way they want to!

COMING SOON TO A CITY NEAR YOU

THE ART OF GLOBAL WARMING

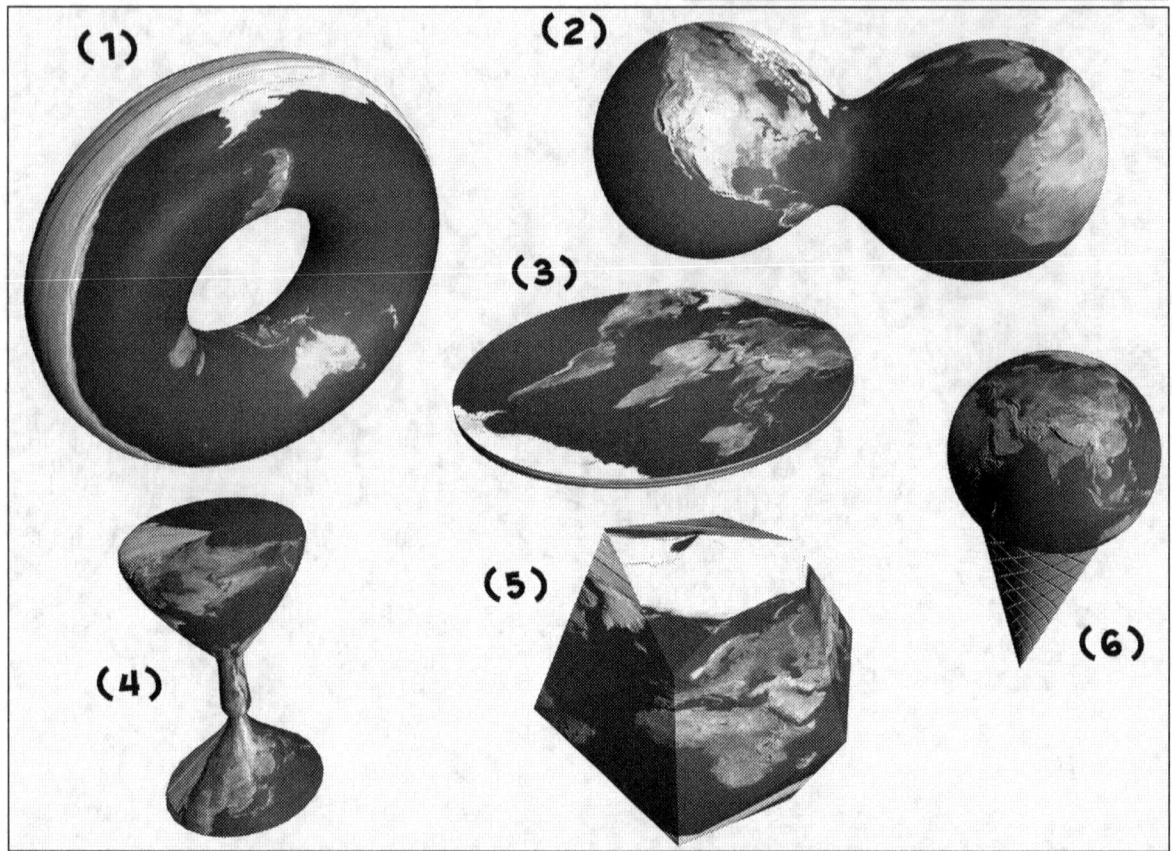

Early Attempts at Designing Earth

In the beginning a number of different designs were proposed for Earth. All of these were rejected for various reasons and the final design was a simple sphere. They were rejected for the following reasons:

(1) *The doughnut* - rejected because the shape was too tempting for large scavenger aliens who have a taste for giant pastries.

(2) *The twister* - originally thought to be useful to separate warring nations but too hard to keep spinning within a stable orbit without bouncing into the sun.

(3) *The Flat Earth* - Originally successful but abandoned because some designers could not help making flat earth jokes, angering the supervisor.

(4) *The wine glass* - specifically designed to appease party animals. The design was discarded when drinking driving limits were to be enforced for space cadets.

(5) *The weird shaped thing* - too many problems were encountered when people kept cutting themselves on the sharp edges. This was abandoned very early.

(6) *The ice cream cone* - a very successful design until the crispy cone got too toasted by the sun. The cone was removed, leaving the Earth as a simple sphere.

The students in Planet School learn about Greenhouse Gas

It is important that today's school children learn about global warming and the effect of greenhouse gas. They can only learn this stuff by understanding the history of the universe. A brief history of the universe goes back about ten million years or so, and every child will probably enjoy the trip down memory lane.

A scene as Salvador Dali would have painted it depicting the effect of global warming on Earth. The elephants march round and round flattening the earth a little more with each journey. There is no end in sight.

John Adlersparre '06

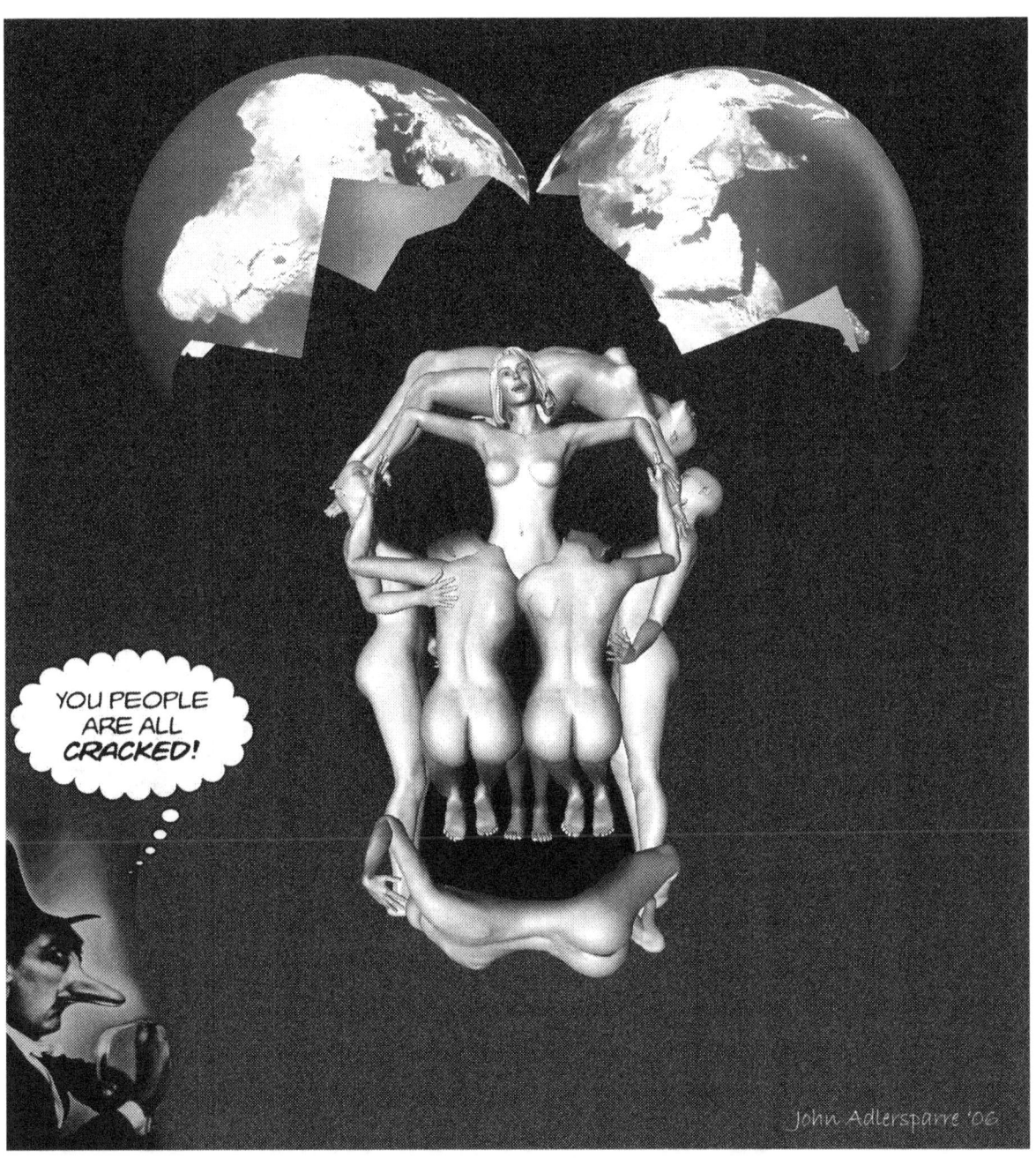

Salvador Dali would have painted his skull this way to bring forth the horrors of the damage done to a fragile planet. The people are blissfully unaware of the impossible situation in which they find themselves.

Vincent Van Gogh would have painted his bedroom this
way to show the dramatic effects of global warming.

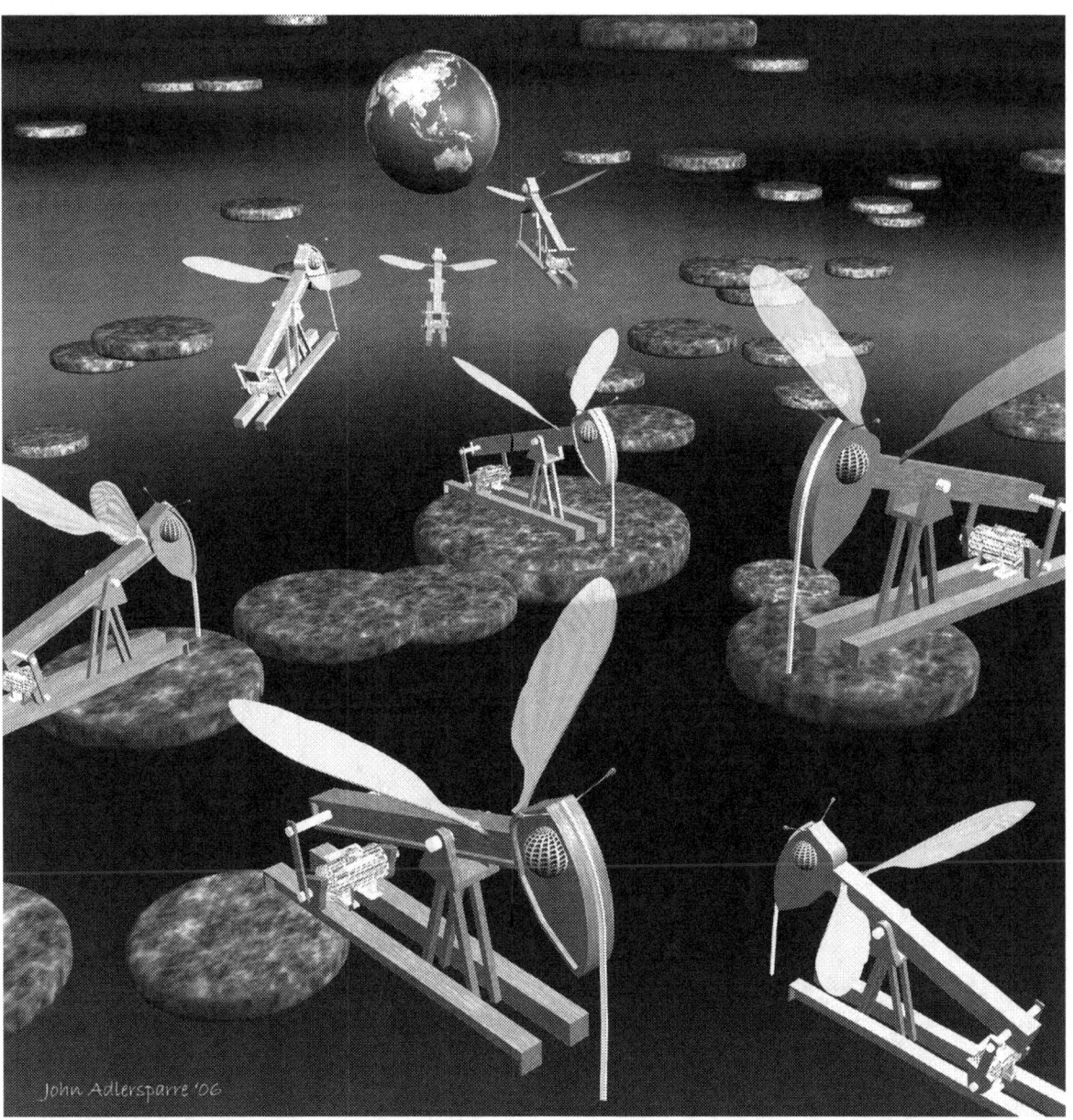

Gradually the thirsty oil bugs make their way through the solar system, depleting every trace of oil from rocks and asteroids. Eventually they move on to whole planets, sucking out the oil and leaving a flattened mass in place of each one. Humans on Earth revere the mystical oil bugs, and build working statues in their likeness hoping they will leave. There is no prevention for the insatiable thirst of the oil bugs. Thus far, with all the money spent on inventing ways to stop their evil progress, humans have only managed to burn up a few trillion gallons of oil with little success.

John Adlersparre '06

Extreme global warming causes the oil monster's shell to lose its outer skin.

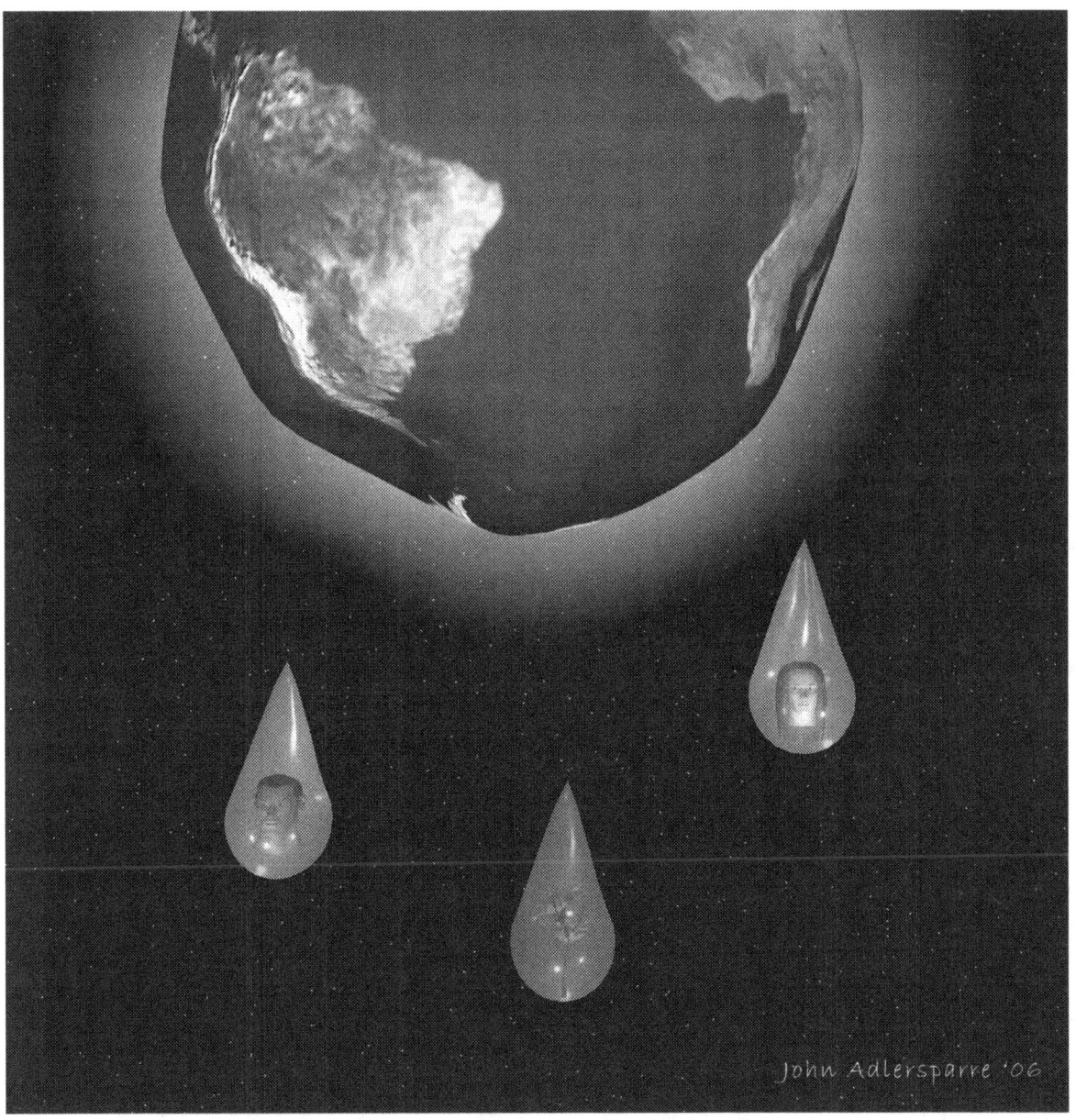

Great scientists and philosophers tell us that the only choice left for civilization is to migrate out to other planets. Of course before we can do this, we need to have the ability to travel trillions of miles at light speed and we need to know just where these other planets are. But it is not necessary for great minds to deal with such trivia, merely to point out that civilization should migrate soon to survive. Governments will be able to help with the travel details by setting up dozens of committees and inventing all manner of new taxes to deal with their never ending thirst for cash.

THE ICE FLOATS AWAY IN ANTARCTICA

"THE LINK BETWEEN GLOBAL WARMING,
GREENHOUSE GAS AND MAN HAS
ALWAYS BEEN UNCLEAR"

World famous cartoonist Adrian Raeside shows us
how global warming affects the planet!

Scientific Hot Flashes

Scientists Discover Global Warming Bacteria

By Dr. Fein Feinstein
The Princeton University Bug Files

Scientists at the Princeton Bug Lab have discovered a previously unknown bacteria whose characteristics clearly indicate that it must be responsible for global warming.

Detailed studies of the new bacteria show that under certain circumstances, heat is generated in fairly large amounts by the complex cells.

Scientists have conducted experiments using different forms of energy to see the resulting effect. It would seem that there are several different energy sources that trigger the bacteria to generate heat.

The bacteria are so prolific, being present almost everywhere, that when bombarded with the known energy sources, they can affect the atmospheric temperature quite a lot.

So far it seems that loud noise and flashing lights cause the most amount of heat generation. Other forms of energy trigger the heat, but not quite as much. Radiation and carbon dioxide just kill the bacteria, so they are not a cause.

The most significant temperature rises have been recorded at or near rock concerts where the surrounding temperature can rise as much as 25 degrees within a few hours. Other sources include cars, planes and people who talk too loud.

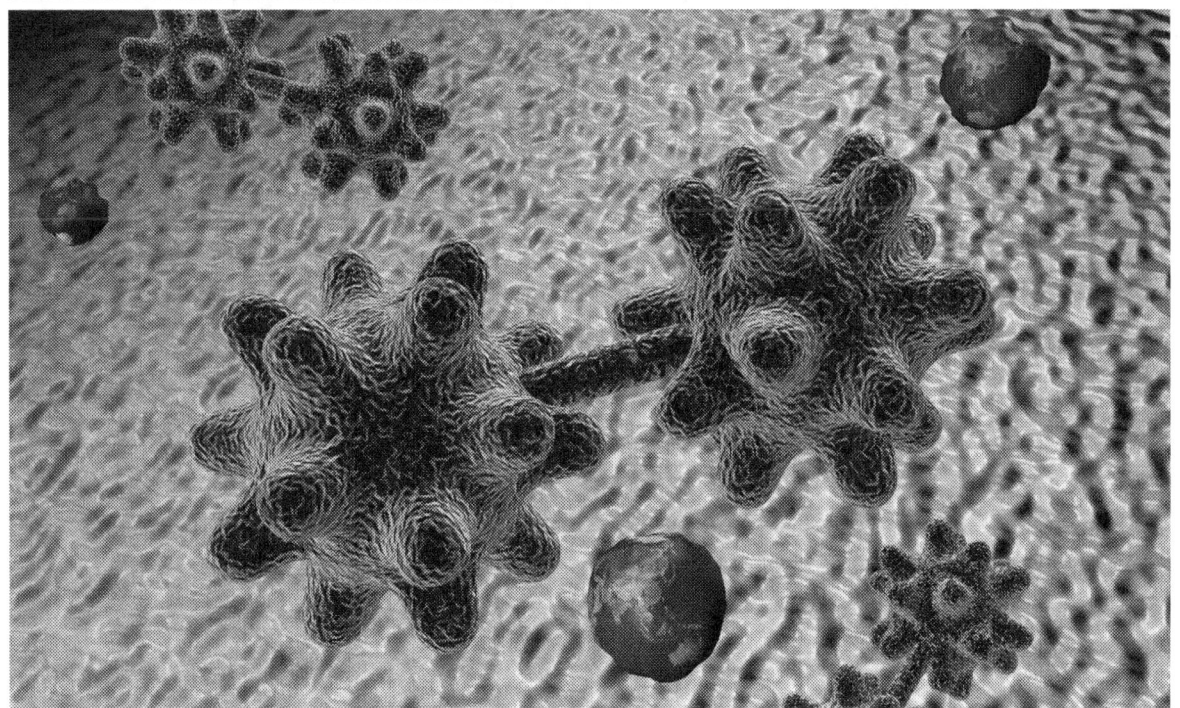

Global warming bacteria shown magnified under an electron microscope

Scientists Discover Links Between Pyramids And Global Warming

By Ra Van Raamsglyph
Pyramids West News Service

It was a lucky day for environmental archaeologists studying the origins of global warming at the Great Pyramids at Giza in the Egyptian desert. Using atomic drills to burrow 100 meters into the Great Pyramid scientists came upon a large room looking somewhat like a well used dining room. Incredibly they found a door that opened to the outside. Apparently pilferers had constructed it in order to steal many of the treasures located in this dining room area. Fortunately they only took gold and jewels and had missed some significant artifacts found hidden under their discarded sandwich wrappers and other debris.

In particular one artifact was of a cylindrical shape with a circular disk on top. In many ways this device looked like a mini pyramid except that it didn't follow the traditional pyramid shape that ancient Egyptians used to construct houses, cookware and many of the scientific instruments of the time.

"There is no doubt that we have found the original food pyramid."

A lab analysis of this cylindrical artifact indicated that the device contained a secret inner chamber which they discovered is capable of slowly cooling hot liquids to room temperature and similarly warming up cool liquids to the same temperature. Scientists found that the device did not work as well when a circular cap found on the device was left on top. In this case the device had the undesirable effect of keeping hot liquids hot and cool liquids cool.

Two different types of refrigerator devices found in the Pyramid at Giza. Storage caps on top must be removed for devices to work correctly.

Dr. Hamada of the Egyptian global warming research Institute conjectured that the cylindrical device may have been Egypt's answered to global warming. Since the device can make cool things warm and warm things cool it was thought that the pyramids were but giant versions of this small experimental device.

Special documents found in another part of the room confirmed Dr. Hamada's idea. One map in fact showed a giant Pyramid full of food. It was thought that the pyramids were intended to serve as large food stores and shelters for the people of Egypt.

Despite this compelling evidence, skeptics still weren't sure.

"If Dr. Hamada's theories were true," they said, "then where is all the food and why are there not more food chambers inside the pyramid?" Dr. Hamada's answer was that they simply did not have time to finish the project. Documents found near another pyramid lent credence to his arguments. Drawings of Egyptians pulling giant slabs of butter towards the pyramids linked up all the theories in a credible way.

The Pyramids are now thought to have been giant cooling mansions which acted very much like refrigerators keeping food at a steady temperature in the hot global warming sun.

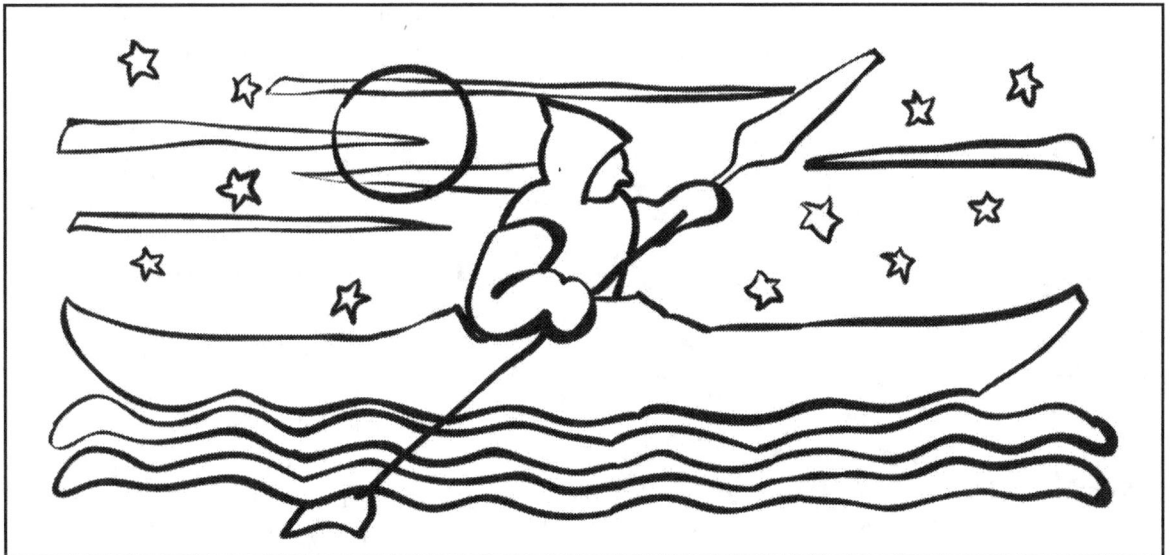

"I'm damn sure there's some ice around here somewhere!"

TRULY AMAZING PET STORIES

Harry and Lisa Finklestein of **Haifa, Israel** wrote to tell us of their unusual cat Otis. It seems that Otis reacts to climate change with incredible consistency, but she does it 24 hours in advance. If the temperature will go up the next day, Otis meows twice each time. For colder, she meows once. And she meows every hour on the hour.

The Finklesteins have done their own research and documented the temperature each day. Otis has never been wrong. They have been measuring this performance for over a year now and have finally decided that Otis might be of great interest to the scientific community.

Unfortunately no researchers seemed particularly thrilled by Otis' magic, even though Harry and Lisa's research showed that the temperature goes up the next day more often than it goes down.

Unfortunately frustration finally took over the Finklestein household and Otis had to be given away. She has been replaced by a dog, Roofey, who only barks at research scientists, and that suits Harry and Lisa just fine.

Alaskans Slap Tax On Cruise Ships

By Captain Svein Pederson
The Cruise News

JUNEAU, AK—Alaskan voters have delivered a stern warning to the cruise ship industry after passing a package of tax and environmental regulations aimed squarely at passenger ships in Alaska waters, citing their ever increasing effect on global warming.

Cheering passengers caught in action near the Hubbard glacier

In a state primary election ballot, Alaskans approved a citizen initiative that will assess a $50 tax on each cruise passenger and tax the cruise lines' corporate earnings and any other revenues collected when the ships are in Alaska waters.

"The Hubbard glacier is like an ice-pack for all our headaches."

The initiative also requires cruise ships to sail only along dotted lines on the water near the shore and adhere to all global warming regulations set forth. Salty Greengrab, Executive Director of the "Tax Everything In Alaska" committee and several of his co-workers have been on numerous cruises with the various cruise lines and have drawn several conclusions why the new tax package is a must.

Discarding the scientific results presented last year by the "Tax Everything In Alaska Through Science" committee, Greengrab stated that science is a waste of time and taxes can easily be justified using more intelligent political minds.

"The warmer it gets, the more we can tax!"

Greengrab and his cohorts have implemented several new fines to be applied to the cruise ships as a matter of course. For example, they noticed that when near the Hubbard glacier, people on the ships cheered whenever large chunks of ice fell off the glacier into the water. Greengrab now wants to fine each person who cheers $5 each time they do it, to stop them from being so happy about the melting.

"Furthermore," said Greengrab, "we believe that the cheering is actually causing more ice to fall off the glacier, so our committee now thinks that the passengers are contributing to global warming."

There is no doubt the citizens of Alaska are firmly behind the new taxation because they can see the results of more cash infusion. There is, however some question about the real reasons behind it all.

This reporter asked a dozen people just how

serious they felt the global warming problem is, and all changed the subject to how the famous Red Dog Saloon in Juneau with the fake sawdust floor could now afford a real sawdust floor without the concrete layer underneath.

Asked what the effect of all this would be on the cruise ship industry in general, Greengrab replied "Hey, my job is to protect the environment and use any method available to do it. Even if it means we have to collect more taxes so we can go on hundreds more cruises around the world to study this warming stuff."

"Global Warming hogwash! I challenge anybody to show me just one place where this plastic globe is melting!"

"I'm sure the researchers will see you, but what makes you think you know anything about global warming?"

Thousands of Research Scientists Protest Canadian Cartoon Book

By Buck Bullstein
NY City News

A typical band of scientist thugs protesting in Washington

WASHINGTON, DC—Roving gangs of enraged marchers thundered through the streets of Washington.

Hundreds of thousands of research scientists and government workers were demonstrating in a mass rally that insiders say may have been one of the biggest ever on Capitol Hill.

Scientists from around the world joined in to protest a Canadian cartoon book depicting that Global Warming could be a joke.

They were seen trying to throw rocks through the windows of the Washington Post building, who's staff first published the cartoon book. Most of the scientists were simply not fit enough to lift the heavy rocks, so they just marched on. Thousands of scientists were also seen trying to burn various Canadian embassies to the ground. Apparently they were unaware that steel fences and cement blocks don't burn very easily.

Protest signs were everywhere. Some of the signs said "Bull for Bucks" while others said "Bucks for Bull." One nude scientist was seen running down the road while being chased by several hundred policemen. The protestor was carrying a sign saying "I like my Mom." However the police soon had the situation under control as they encircled the man and started to beat him with copies of Scientific American Magazine.

> **"We cannot allow all these scientific hooligans to run wild and annoy our citizens."**

Dr. Kyoto from the Kyoto Accord took the microphone and told the protestors that this was a momentous day for Global Warming. He emphasized that it was important to obtain lucrative government grant money before the ice caps melted, thus eliminating the key data source, ice core samples, used to confound the government to obtain truck loads of money to study Global Warming.

Dr. Kyoto, also known as "The Imperial Emperor of Global Warming", urged the crowd to remain calm. He stated that his speech to burn down the Canadian embassies was only meant in a figurative sense. This time he advocated a counter cartoon campaign showing the burning of Canada as a result of Global Warming.

The protest ended at 5:00 p.m. sharp when many of the protestors were hungry and went to MacDonal's to eat. Being dissatisfied with the slow service, protesters threatened to trash several MacDonal's establishments by knocking over the trash cans. Unfortunately for them, most were too tired from all the marching, and so they simply sat down and ate when their orders were ready.

OOPS! A CORRECTION

In a previous article we stated that the color of farmed salmon is determined by the type of food they eat. This is incorrect. In actual fact, the color of farmed salmon is changing with the temperature fluctuations caused by global warming. As the temperature goes up, they get more red. We apologize if anyone was confused by this. - ed.

"Great! Now we have to do a snow dance for a bunch of flakes who have messed up our climate!"

Global Warming Research Documents Disappear From Libraries

By Joseph Liberatio
The West City News

WASHINGTON, DC—Researchers and students have reported several times in recent weeks that there is a mysterious lack of information about Global Warming. It seems that related documents, previously available in most libraries across the city, are gradually disappearing.

"But it's not just theft," says Arthur Molenester, a student at The George Washington University. Molenester is studying the effects of global warming on ostriches, and has a lucrative research grant that depends heavily on such information being available. In each reference section where there should have been a research paper or other document, there is instead a piece of paper simply marked "Withheld".

Molenester as well as other students and researchers are asking, "who is withholding the information, and why?"

Certain aspects of the mystery are beginning to make more sense, according to Elizabeth Anklenoor, head

librarian at the Scientific Reference Division of the Library of Congress. "This follows the same pattern as other so-called sensitive documents," said Anklenoor. This seems to go hand in hand with the recent declaration by the feds and the oil cartel that it [global warming] is a non-issue. So it would seem that by hiding the research information, they hope to make the problem go away.

But Molenester and his fellow students are not giving up that easily. His group has systematically gone through thousands of reference publications and pasted false labels over them so the feds cannot find them. It seems to work since the loss of reference material has dropped significantly.

"Libraries are a source of information, not a secret society!"

"It's easy" said Molenester, "all we have to do is print a phony title on a strip of transparent tape and stick it on the publication." So far the most successful title that throws the feds off is 'Efficient Ways to Make Government Work Well', apparently enough to scare away even the most dedicated feds, but other titles seem to work well too.

"On the other hand," he continued, "we have tried putting titles about global warming on boring

publications and they disappear within a few days." This, it would seem, is an ideal way to clear outdated and other unwanted materials from the library without incurring any additional expense.

Molenester remains convinced that the problem is more like a horrible video game.

Fun at the oil company picnic

Scientists Develop Time Tracking Method To Measure Climate Changes

By Arthur Dismantle
The Daily Express Journal

LONDON, ENGLAND—Scientists at the Geoffrey Puddncake Institute in London have developed an amazing way to literally go back in time to measure climate changes very precisely. This information will allow much more accurate predictions of when the Earth will become uninhabitable.

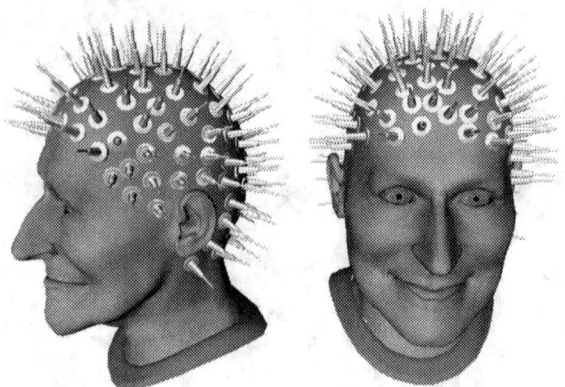

Early alpha and beta brain wave electrodes now made obsolete by new technology

There are two basic principles of science that lead to the device that makes this all possible. First, it is a widely known fact that when people are hypnotized, they can be taken back to past lives and can recall and relate events that happened in past lives. This is referred to as Hypnotic Regression.

Second, every living person emits strong alpha and beta brain waves that can be measured and recorded. These brain waves can now be analyzed and converted with computers into text and video information. Combining the two principles, a machine has been developed that will replay all the activity for every living person, and will display that information as a series of running videos.

In order to capture brain waves without inconveniencing anybody, large radio towers are being constructed all over the world. To cover more remote areas, extremely powerful satellites are being launched and pointed at the people in those areas. Eventually it is hoped that only satellites will be used everywhere so that people will not need to worry about the ever-present monitoring stations. The early brain wave electrodes pictured here are no longer needed.

With some very clever post-processing software, all the video information can be recombined and followed using a machine called an Event Back Tracker, or EBT. The EBT provides a search capability by date and location, so that any event involving a person that has ever happened before in their present or any past life, anywhere on the planet can be directly accessed and replayed.

> **"By going back in time we can watch every event that has ever occurred anywhere."**

Once all this information is available, scientists can observe people looking at thermometers and barometers, and record what they are seeing and how they dress for the climate each day. Other events, like winter or spring arriving can be observed and recorded for years at a time.

The technology has a lot of practical applicability in other areas. Major Norton Crumcracker, co-chairman of the Joint Climate Group suggests that he might finally be able find his missing research information and umbrella, lost many months ago.

He's is hoping this will put him back on track to complete his urgent research paper.

Meanwhile the American FBI couldn't help but notice the considerable advantages of going back in time and observing everything people have done all their lives, and even during their past lives.

Thousands of unsolved cases can now be investigated and criminals can be prosecuted for crimes going back literally hundreds of years ago. The government is discussing building much larger jails for all the miscreants.

The United States Internal Revenue Service (the tax department) is anxious to partake of this technology to chase down and recover hundreds of millions of dollars in unreported revenue.

Lawyers throughout the world are busily inventing reasons why courts should reject actual video of events as they happen. They are trying to convince judges not to convict people for crimes committed tens of decades ago by people when they were somebody else in a past life.

Civil rights groups and other activists are having a field day protesting everything they can think of relating to this new science.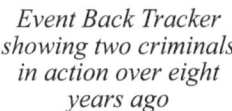

Event Back Tracker showing two criminals in action over eight years ago

Latest Global Warming Interest survey. This issue!

Experiment Fails In Ukraine

Scientists in the Ukraine were feverishly putting the last touches on a huge ion collider designed to collect particles from the atmosphere, and then shoot them into space.

As a result of this action, particles responsible for warming up the planet would be systematically eliminated and the planet would cool down once again.

That was the theory, however, theories don't always work in practice.

A large group of dignitaries and citizens gathered at the main laboratory, as scientists prepared the master switch to the sound of bands and singing choirs. The switch was thrown and with a flash, the entire laboratory and everyone near it simply disappeared.

Apparently the ion collider had created a black hole, sucking in everything around it.

Local mayor Opuk Bakotska declared that every Monday, residents will spend the day searching for the black hole to find lost citizens.

"Professor Zitkin suddenly realizes that he has created the perfect Global Warming model."

Pineapple Culprit Behind Global Warming

By Laimana Keoni
The Pineapple Express

HILO, HI—Just as meteorologists exhale after a very grueling two weeks of severe winter weather in the western and central United States, scientists have identified one of the leading causes of the bad weather. Incredibly their findings also explain Global Warming as we currently understand it. "The leading climate culprit is now known to be nothing more than the common pineapple," said Wayne Higgins, lead climate specialist at the National Climate Prediction Center.

Typical guilty pineapple

"Pineapples dipped in chlorine to preserve them are reacting with the environment."

Apparently the common pineapple contains wet yellow juices, which are thought to have a disturbing influence on the climate. Scientists are well aware that pineapples suck up a huge amount of moisture out of the atmosphere during their nine-month incubation period. By the time the pineapples hatch, nearly 50% of the atmospheric moisture contained in the clouds around Hawaii are gone. This in turn causes a heating effect that we refer to as Global Warming. By early January 2006, this lack of precipitation associated with the "pineapple effect" extended into the western tropical Pacific.

As the tropical dryness associated with the pineapple effect shifted eastward towards the Central tropical Pacific, jet planes which deliver this precious cargo to the United States Government for their dinner parties further added to the Global Warming problem by emitting huge clouds of white smoke into the upper stratosphere.

This smoke is also thought to be the cause of the greenhouse effect. The greenhouse effect prevents pineapples from achieving their typically golden color. Thus pineapples remain somewhat green. Consequently this affects the American pineapple economy, as people no longer can distinguish between real and artificial pineapples.

The typical pineapple is shown in the above photo accompanying this article. The greenhouse effect can be seen particularly well on the pineapple leaves. The US government has quickly responded to the Global Warming crisis by imposing a pineapple tax on residents of Hawaii while at the same time cracking down on boatloads of Mexicans who smuggle pineapples from Hawaii into Florida.

These measures should in theory reduce the need for pineapples other than for state sponsored parties and therefore more moisture will be retained in the atmosphere, thus reducing Global Warming to a large extent. This government action may however result in months of heavy rain and cause possible flooding of the ocean surrounding Hawaii.

The "pineapple effect" is so named because pineapples are now largely considered to be the primary cause of global warming. Meteorologists now refer to this warming as the "Pineapple Express".

Pineapple with moisture measuring instruments

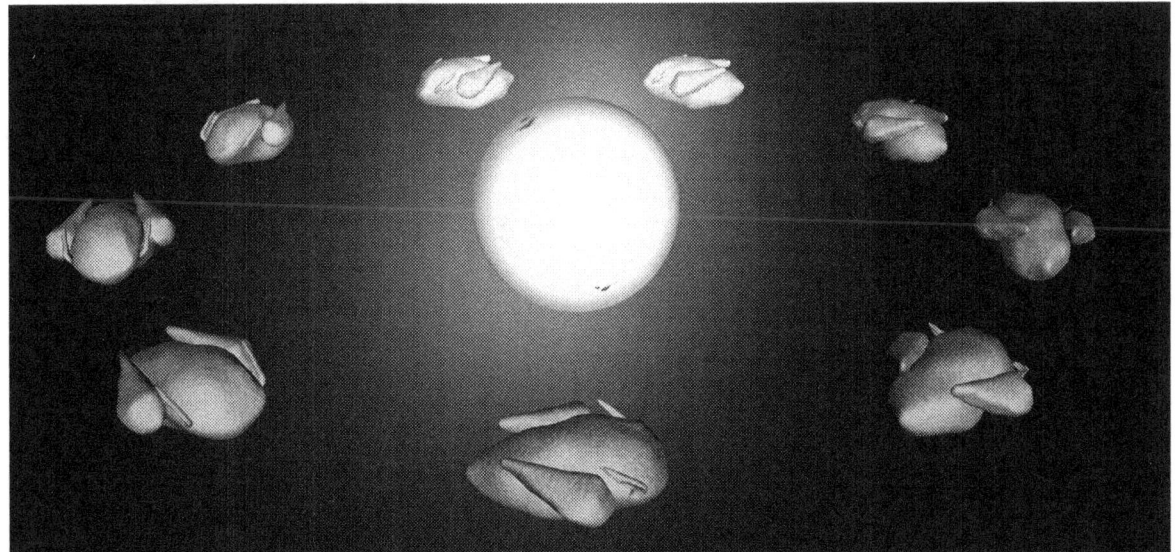

Understanding The Climate

The planets can be thought of as barbecued chickens, rotating around a hot fire. As they heat up, they get cooked until ready to serve. If chickens are under cooked, there is a danger that eating them will give you a stomach ache. If they are left to cook too long, they will burn to charcoal, and charcoal is considered toxic so it should not be eaten.

Thus the chicken should be served when it is cooked to perfection. Now some people like to add barbecue sauces to make the chicken taste better. But sometimes the sauces will burn and cause a lot of smoke that smells bad. It can also make you cough and your eyes will water. So it is really best to forget about the sauce, and just enjoy the normal cooking process. Now you understand how the climate works!

Scientists Protest The Size Of Government Grants

By Ray Cashcrop
The GlobalWarming News Daily

ANTWERP, BELGIUM—In a surprise move to protest the miniature size of government grants, scientists from around the world have decided on a one day protest by coming to work with their hair uncombed.

Industry insiders say it's really disgusting how professional scientists could do such a thing. Other's however say they don't see any difference, in that they always look like that.

Dr. Hairgenhoffer

Apparently Albert Einstein set the hair trend back in the 1950's and it has stuck ever since. Dr. Hairgenhoffer of the European Global Warming consortium, shown above, said that really his hair is not as combed as before.

If the government does not increase the size of grants then scientists from around the world will increase the pressure by coming to work without their faces washed.

They vaguely hinted that with such poor grooming, they could not be held responsible for inaccurate research and possible mistakes made during their experiments. Companies, they said, should be aware that it might cost more to correct mistakes if the research is not done properly because they are forced to not comb their hair, making them unable to see what they are doing.

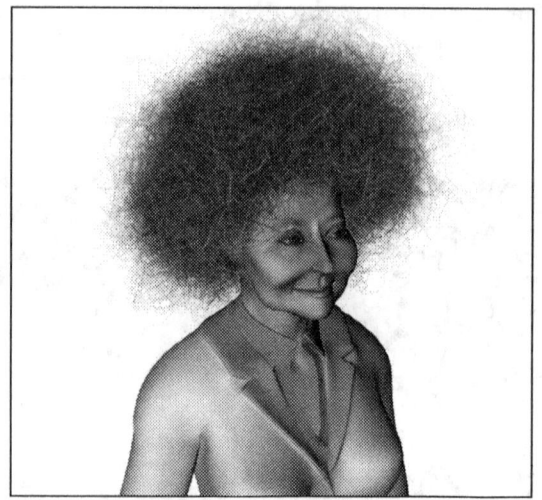
Frieda Hairgenhoffer

CNN contacted Dr. Hairgenhoffer's wife Frieda Hairgenhoffer to see what she thought about the whole thing. She said, "really I can't remember the last time he washed his face. He's so busy with this global warming stuff every day."

Dr. Hairgenhoffer hopes that the government standoff will end soon because he would hate to escalate even more and come to work without brushing his teeth.

Canada Ratifies Kyoto Treaty

DELICIOUS, EH?

OTTAWA, ONTARIO—The Government of Canada today announced its ratification of the Kyoto Protocol to the United Nations Framework Convention on Climate Change. This follows votes by members of the House of Commons and Senate in favour of ratification, a process for making all documents edible.

"The United Nations and the International Food Consortium have worked hard for nine years to achieve international agreement on a global framework for action," said Foreign Affairs Consultant Bill Rat. "In the Speech from the Throne, the Government of Canada committed to ratifying the Protocol before the end of the year and

---

"Ratifying a document gives one a very precarious sense of satisfaction."

---

today we met that commitment."

At the United Nations Headquarters in New York City, where he delivered the instrument of ratification, Environment Minister David Rat said, "Ratifying the Kyoto Protocol is the right thing to do for Canadians, for the global environment and for future generations. The scientific consensus demanded action, and the Government of Canada listened and worked with all sectors and segments of the population to develop an edible Climate Change Plan for Canada that will taste delicious."

"Ratification is an important milestone in Canada's contribution to addressing climate change as an edible document. Now, we can look forward to the next challenge of the implementation phase," said Natural Resources Minister Herb Rat. "The Climate Change Plan for Canada provides a delicious framework for action and we will continue to build on this through ongoing consultations with provinces, territories, and food manufacturers in the months and years ahead."

The Climate Change Plan for Canada symbolizes a national goal—for Canadians to become the most sophisticated and efficient consumers and producers of edible documents in the world and leaders in the development of new, more appealing document flavours.

Flavors tested and approved so far include maple, beer, chocolate and bacon - always used as flavors in other basic food group types such as milk shakes, pizzas and meat pie tourtiere from Quebec.

Earth

Sun

The Global Warming scream

Medics May Declare New Addition To Endangered Species List

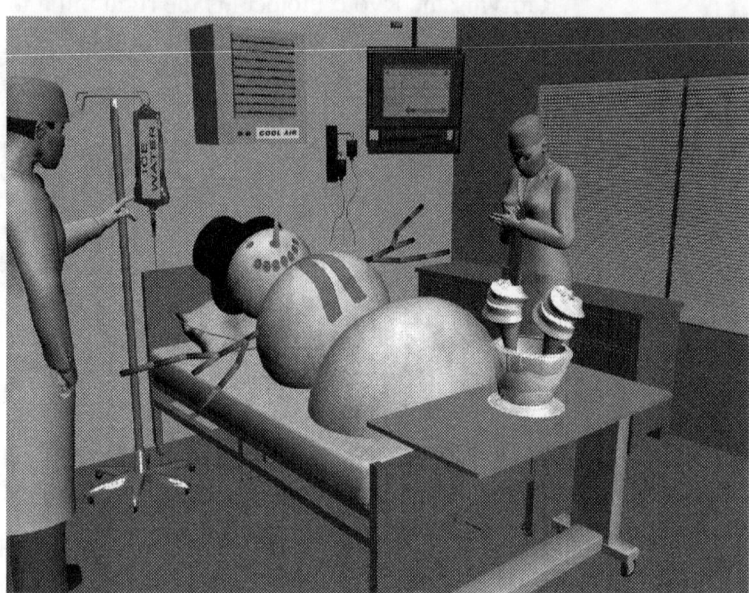

By Whitey Flakeman
Fairbanks News

FAIRBANKS, AK—There is more bad news coming from environmentalists and researchers at the North Pole.

Dr. Henry Frosterno, chief medical officer at the Fairbanks Memorial Hospital today announced that several snowmen have been admitted to the hospital for emergency treatment. Dr. Frosterno estimated about a dozen arrived just this week.

"The people have to pull together to fight this new climate menace..."

The prognosis does not look good. In spite of every effort to cool down the snowmen to prevent them from melting, nature is unfortunately taking its course. "We have tried everything from intravenous ice water to bringing in heavy duty deep freezers, but nothing seems to help" said Frosterno.

The next step is for the research team at the hospital to analyze the results of tests. No x-rays are permitted because of the fear that the snowmen could be further melted in the process. Carl Lookalot, senior research scientist at the hospital is optimistic that a solution can be found. Lookalot declared "we will get to the bottom of this. None of those guys are leaving my hospital in a bucket."

Word about the dilemma has reached far and wide, particularly since a lot of children are going to suffer indirectly as a result of the loss of their snowmen. Singer-actor ICE-T has hinted that he might put a concert together to garner funding for more sophisticated and expensive research.

Not to be outdone in this critical time of need, the Alaska state governor has declared a state-wide day of hope and celebration, encouraging all residents to make ice cubes and bring them to the hospital.

Nobody wants to face the reality proposed by local scientist E.J. Snufflaker. He has declared that global warming is the cause of the whole problem. And he bases this conclusion on the ongoing pollution created by snowmobilers racing on Nuk Iklook's Fun-In-The-Snow ranch. Other government researchers simply pass this off as a continuation of the long feud between Iklook and Snufflaker, who has been banned from the ranch for allegedly failing to use the proper facilities, resulting in numerous yellow snow episodes. "Global warming" said one government fossil fuel researcher, when asked last week, "is just a figment of your imagination."

Nevertheless there seems to be a very real problem. It will be another four or five weeks before any conclusive results can be determined from the tests. Until then, children are encouraged to treat snowmen with respect and above all, don't offer them any hot chocolate.

"I know we're having a global warming crisis, but do you have to lay hard-boiled eggs?"

OVERHEARD IN AN ELEVATOR

"My company can get away with murder now that the Kyoto agreement is history!"

Greenhouse Gas A Blessing For Car Industry

Scientists have come up with an ingenious idea that may be an answer to global warming and the ever growing problem of environmental damage caused by greenhouse gas. Dr. Carnoff, who developed the idea, works at the Ford motor company development plant in Detroit. He said that his idea is really just an extension of research done for the battery powered fuel efficient cars that now consume huge amounts of Hydrogen gas.

GreenGas

"Overpriced fuel will soon be a thing of the past."

Essentially Dr. Carnoff has designed and built an engine that runs on greenhouse gas. "This kind of fuel is everywhere. It is abundant in the atmosphere," said Dr. Carnoff. "So why not make use of it?" He then said that we would essentially kill two birds with one stone if his solution was implemented on a massive worldwide scale.

On the one hand it would decrease our dependence on gasoline powered vehicles and on the other hand it would extract dangerous greenhouse gasses such as CO2 from the atmosphere resulting in far cleaner air.

Existing gas stations can be converted to greenhouse gas processing units that extract greenhouse gas from the air, purify it and then pump it into the new fuel efficient and ergonomically attractive Hi IQ Cars. To the average consumer, it would be life as normal with gas stations looking almost the same.

Dr. Carnoff's idea is very simple as well as practical and futuristic. Output from the cars is pure H2O or water. An unforeseen side benefit is that the water output will automatically keep the roads clean and protect them from global heat cracking problems.

When asked if there were any negative points to the new proposed scheme, Dr. Carnoff said that he couldn't foresee any problems, at least not in the long run. For the short term existing oil and gas reserves would still be used to run the greenhouse gas purification units, but those are expected to require less fuel than the millions of cars on the roads today.

Dr. Carnoff expected that in the future, the greenhouse purification units may very well use an alternate energy source that is as yet unforeseen.

President Bush was very happy with the excellent work done by Dr. Carnoff and his large research staff. Dr. Carnoff's colleagues said they would be surprised if he did not receive this year's Nobel Prize for environmental research.

Shown to the left is an artist's rendering of the new gas powered greenhouse gas purification unit which can be installed on top of existing gas pumps. Greenhouse gas is fed into the back of the unit to produce a cleaner blue colored fuel.

Town Becomes First To Enforce "Smart" Sizes To Combat Global Warming

By Arvid Wiss
The Smartville Daily

SMARTVILLE, NV—Smartville is a town full of smart residents. By an overwhelming vote of 20-3 the town council ruled that all vehicles, buildings and just about everything else in the town will adhere to strict climate-friendly sizes.

"There is absolutely no limit to how smart we can get."

All buildings are to be torn down and replaced with smart structures that are only about one quarter the size of the original buildings. All vehicles are to be sold and replaced with new "smart" vehicles.

Special redesign requests have been sent to all the major auto manufacturers to build smart cars and trucks.

Exciting new auto design changes include soft-sided vehicles to fit even the most portly drivers, and many styles to choose from, including smart SUV's and smart pickup trucks.

Using smart vehicles and living in smart buildings, the town council estimates the pollution normally created by the town will decrease by more than 20%. Citizens will be told how many times their property taxes will multiply to cover the extra costs for all the changes.

"This encourages a healthier life style through weight loss."

Special recognition will be given to auto commuters who can fit more than one person in their vehicle.

Meanwhile the local Smartville police insist there is absolutely no truth to the rumor that local unsavory character Tony Baritone has made veiled threats against anyone who tries to change the size of his muscle car.

More Mystery Towers Found In North America

By Lydia Snoopmeister
The Lonely Cove Chatterbox

LONELY COVE, NS—Residents of this rural farm area are wondering just what the strange towers that are cropping up are intended for. Several have been sighted in an area of just a few square miles, on both public and private property.

Tower at Zeb Zeberson's farm in Lonely Cove

Local government officials, when asked to find out what the towers are used for, reluctantly replied that the official name for them is "Global Warming Observation Stations." But using the freedom of information process, we have found a diagram that seems to disagree with this explanation. When received, the diagram had obviously been edited for content.

Scene from helicopter over Lonely Cove Golf Club

The satellite dishes all around each tower appear to be designed to intercept cell and regular phone transmissions, while the observatory at the top can only be described as a way of spying on the general population.

"These towers hide something, we're going to find out what..."

But you be the judge. When grilled by the Lonely Cove town council why the towers are being built in towns and rural areas, the federal representative replied "You people just can't be expected to comprehend the effects of Global Warming, so just assume everything is under control."

Residents in subdivisions are becoming concerned about the frequent traffic to and from the towers, mostly large black SUV's with men and women dressed in black wearing very dark glasses. Each vehicle was clearly marked "Department of Homeland Security," although no such department seems to exist in Canada.

"One of our residents is missing. Now it's serious."

Ida Frinklauer, prominent leader of the Lonely Cove Knitting Club, was the first to vocally demand more information about the towers.

Ms. Frinklauer marched into one of the towers requesting an explanation and has not been seen since. Anyone hearing from her is asked to contact

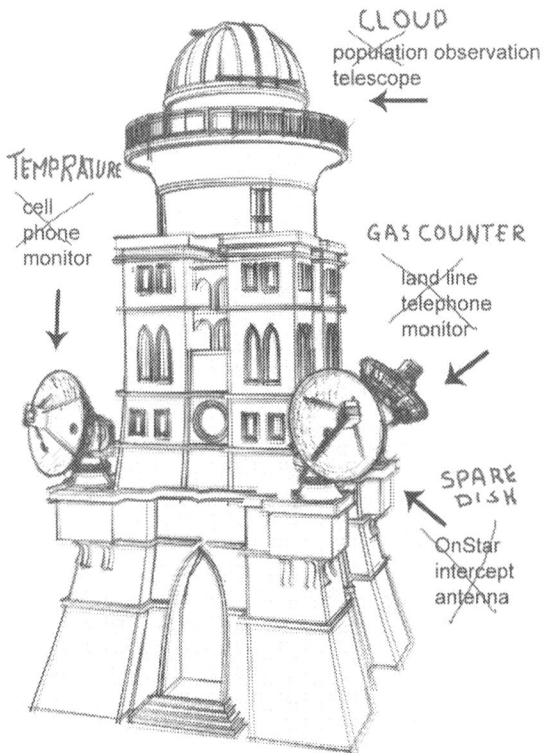

Labels on diagram:
- **CLOUD** ~~population~~ observation telescope
- **TEMPRATURE** ~~cell phone monitor~~
- **GAS COUNTER** ~~land line telephone monitor~~
- **SPARE DISH** ~~OnStar intercept antenna~~

Mystery tower diagram we found through freedom of information showing crudely written changes

the local RCMP immediately. Several citizen groups are forming in an attempt to get to the bottom of the mysterious buildings.

Thus far the explanations have not seemed to satisfy residents or visitors to the area. Until further information is available, this reporter and local radio stations will continue to update you as we find out more.

"Can you dry clean a much larger version of this?"

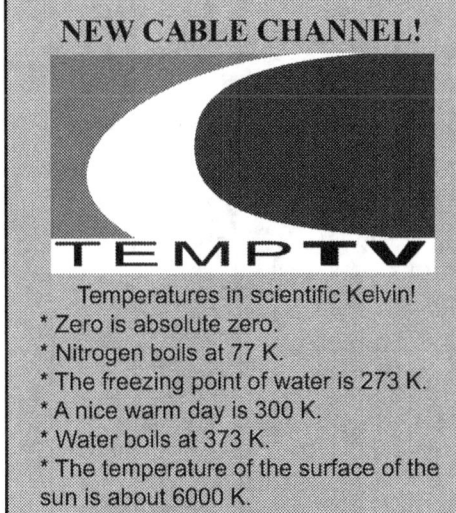
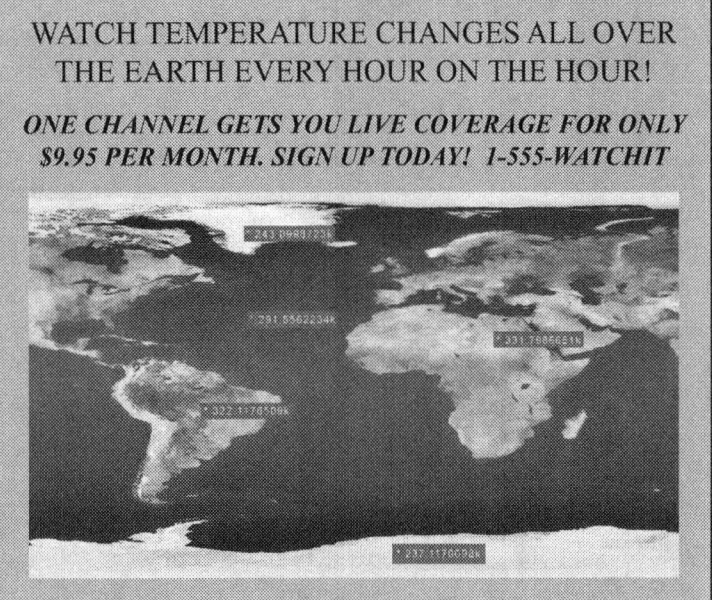

Global Warming Magnetizing People

Are metal items attacking us?

By Nick Tesla
The Journal of South African Metals

CAPE TOWN, SOUTH AFRICA—The rapid changes in climate being measured all over the globe are causing some extra special notice here in South Africa.

It would seem that base metals are undergoing some changes in characteristics. There are many observed so far, but the most significant seems to be the effect some metals are having on us.

So far scientists have examined the basic metals used in everyday applications such as nails, screws and aluminum cans. All three are apparently leeching electrons into the air that are being absorbed by humans and animals.

> ## "Even metals that are not normally magnetic are being attached to people."

There is a much higher percentage of metallic electrons measured in every person and animal tested. It is widely known that metal electrons are attracted to each other from very short distances, but new observations indicate that the attraction has become much wider.

It is believed that this attraction has increased dramatically with the onset of global warming. The attraction distance is no longer measured in nanometers, but rather in hundreds of meters.

Without wanting to get too scientific, we can compare this to a small boy now being able to throw a tennis ball hundreds of miles instead of just a few meters.

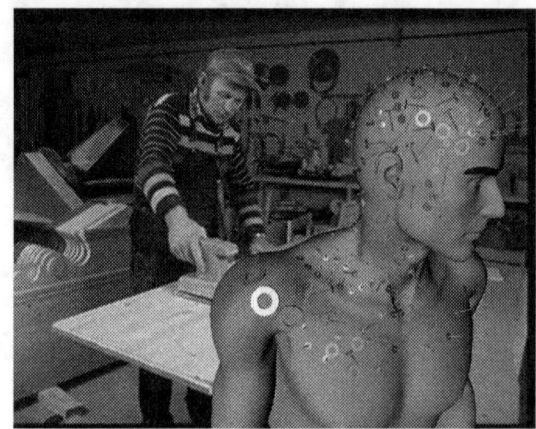

Typical affected carpenter leaves work

So what is the significance of this? Dr. Maxine Planke of the Cape Town Science Club puts it this way: "we have every reason to believe that electrons from metallic objects are invading our bodies and then magnetically sticking themselves to us."

Sound strange enough? Consider the normal actions of a virus. It invades the body, makes some minor alterations and then begins to grow within us. The only difference is that metallic objects are not living organisms,

Aluminum cans on a dog

but they do seem to have some bizarre plan in

mind.

Skeptics were questioning this strange theory until Dr. Planke invited them to take a bus tour with her through some of the more densely populated areas in Cape Town.

There witnesses observed some shocking sights. People were walking around apparently normally, but literally covered in nails, screws and other small metal objects.

Many people are falling victim to this strange affliction, while others seem to be unaffected.

The metal objects can be removed easily without any harm, but whenever one walks near other metal objects, they soon come back.

One interesting effect is the attraction of aluminum, which is not normally attracted to magnets. It seems the same principle is at work and no metals are safe to handle.

As long as the phenomenon continues there are a number of people who can make a tidy living just walking around and attracting metal bits they can resell.

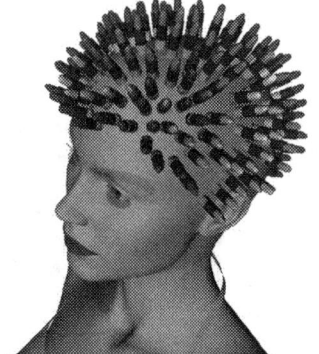

This enterprising young woman makes a fashion statement using colorful lipsticks magnetically attached to her head.

Remarkable Windmill Discovery!

Dutch scientists exploring windmills as a renewable energy source have found that when used as hats, they are capable of generating enough power to transport people over long distances. Commercial manufacturers hope to have affordable models available soon.

New Discovery Reverses Skin Damage Caused By Climate Changes

By Lila Spuften
Modern Makeover Secrets

The skin rejuvenator

DUBLIN, IRELAND—Technology has triumphed one again. With the climate changes going on around us, the temperature is rising and our skin is reacting to the heat.

If you want to get the jump on climate changes to your skin, you can book an appointment at one of the new skin refresher studios. They are opening up in many locations throughout the city.

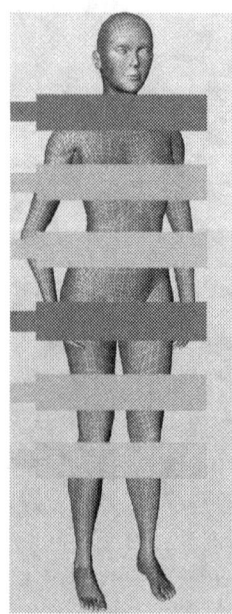

The process is actually quite simple. You lie down in a Global Tube and the system scans your skin from top to bottom. Then the average color is calculated using a 3-D simulation, ignoring hair and other non-skin colors.

Once the scanning has been completed, the results are fed into a colorimeter system that automatically mixes some color paint that exactly matches your original skin color.

The windows on the tube close, and some very fine nozzles spray the paint all around you from head to toe. The color is guaranteed to last at least a month even with frequent showering.

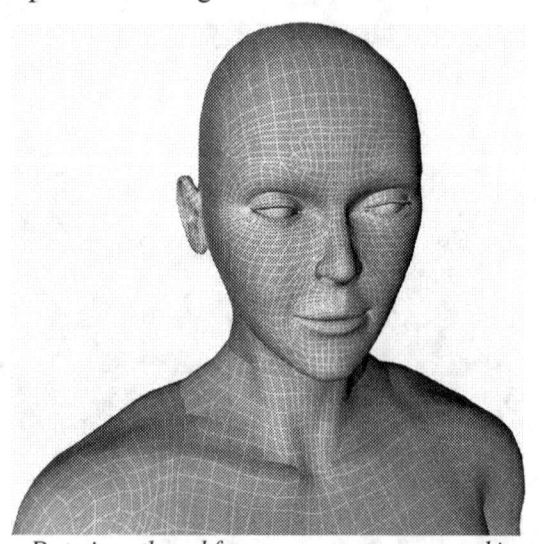

Data is gathered from many spots on your skin

The whole process from start to finish takes a quick three hours and is completely painless. Once the painting is completed, it is recommended that you wait a few hours before wearing wool clothes.

"Apart from a few minor issues this treatment is the perfect body complexion solution."

There are a few minor side effects. For example, you will feel very stiff for a few days while the paint absorbs moisture from your skin and softens. And for a few days you will be quite shiny.

The only other thing to remember after this wonderful skin rejuvenation is that there are some foods you cannot eat. Any fruits or vegetables with extreme colors must be avoided. Eating these types of food will cause your skin to take on the color of the food. Avoid anything red, green or blue, the primary colors. And avoid eating combinations of these since together they can produce a wide spectrum of colors. It's best to restrict your diet to bland colored foods such as pasta, potatoes and transparent jelly fish.

Many more commemorative photos available at the Canadian Federal Archive site!

The Greenhouse Gas Chain - Who's Measuring Whom?

By Fin Waterson
Pacific Ocean Weekly Gazette

PACIFIC OCEAN—Greenhouse gas is a popular topic and getting much hotter as researchers begin to see the huge value in studying the problem further. Japan has recently built and commissioned a scientific ship to go about the oceans of the world and measure everything from pollutants in the air to life forms at the very bottom of the oceans.

> **"Measuring pollution only half way is a sure fire way to cloud the accuracy of the results"**

Air measurements include analyses of air particles, temperature, cloud construction and winds, all of which affect the global climate and contribute to the changes that seem to happen almost daily. It is always sunny in one place while rain might be falling another. This is what the Japan Discovery is all about.

Chief Joe Waters supervises pollution measuring process

Water is thoroughly analyzed too. In fact there is a long list of tests done on samples of water, every hour of the day. Results and conclusions are posted on the internet on various web sites for all to see.

As if studying air and water is not enough, the Discovery also digs down deep into the bottom layers of the ocean to study pollutants and things that live down there to see how they change when the earth's climate changes.

But there is one form of pollution the Discovery isn't measuring - its own. That's where the environmental group Greenfleece stepped in and now follows the Discovery, recording how much toxic smoke is emitted while it moves about the ocean. But Greenfleece's ship emits enough of its own toxic smoke that chief Joe Waters of the Haida First Nation People, in British Columbia Canada, has taken up the responsibility for measuring that ship's emissions.

Not to be left out of the loop, the Canadian government is starting a whole new program with the idea of creating a fresh source of tax money. Researchers have been tasked with measuring how much paint comes off the bottom of ships and canoes, and how the chemicals in it can affect the climate. Ships would be taxed according to how much they affect the climate. The Environment Minister was quoted as saying, "I should get some kind of award for thinking up these things." 🌐

"Do you guys realize that your smoking will cause global warming a million years from now?"

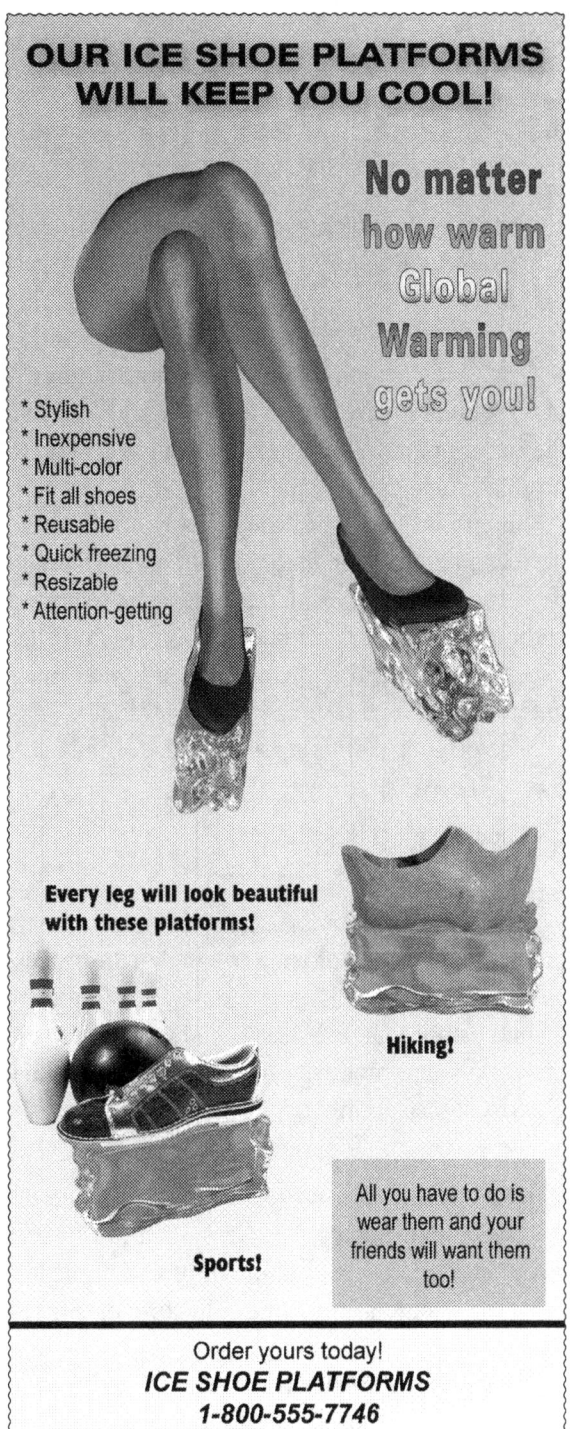

Genetic Plant Mutations Fight Global Warming

By Abderus Phyllotaxis
The National Rainforest Enquirer

AMAZON BASIN, BRAZIL—The word of the day here in Brazil is Photosynthesis. It is widely known that plants take carbon dioxide from the air and water from the ground to produce sugar and oxygen.

Scientists here have been working hard to perfect a new genetic mutation, including a brand new formula for the plants that will use more carbon dioxide at a faster rate. Carbon dioxide is the excessive chemical in the air caused by too much greenhouse gas emissions from fossil fuel.

The original plant photosynthesis formula is:

$$12H_2O + 6CO_2 \text{----------}> C_6H_{12}O_6 + 6O_2$$

The new magic formula is:

$$11H_2O + 12CO_2 \text{----------}> C_{12}H_{22}O_{11} + 12O_2$$

When the formula is inserted into plants, extra molecules of carbon dioxide are used in the process so more of the harmful greenhouse gas is removed from the atmosphere. Virtually the same sugar and more oxygen is produced compared to the original photosynthesis formula.

There is another requirement to make the new formula work well, and scientists have made the necessary adjustments. The sizes of various leaves have been increased significantly to handle the process. People are making adjustments for the new sizes.

Where the original leaves from an Elephant Ear plant might have been about 12 inches across, they are now 10 or more feet across. Other plants have

Tree'ola the magical rain forest king approves the new formula

leaves that are even larger.

The new giant leaves are very useful for a variety of purposes including construction, food and clothing.

The economy of the rainforest area has suddenly taken a very successful jump. Since the leaves are so big, and many areas in other countries are flattened and made into big ugly cities with no space left, the Government has set up a program to ensure huge areas in Brazil will remain as rainforest "cash crop" areas.

"There does not seem to be any limit to the size of leaves we can create with our mutations!"

Through a carefully managed program of positioning plants to point towards the direction around the planet where the carbon dioxide emissions are worst, scientists can maximize the benefits of greenhouse gas removal while ensuring big revenue sources.

They claim the continents creating the heaviest carbon dioxide gas concentrations are North America, Asia, and most of the others. Any country where the gas is produced becomes a potential client for the leaf cleaning service.

Brazil will be able to process much more evil carbon dioxide than any other country, and will be charging a global tax for their services. As more carbon dioxide appears, more huge plants will be grown to handle the excessive gas.

Building in rainforest showing genetic leaf enhancements

"I'm thinking maybe we need a smaller mascot for our Global Warming conference!"

Professor Rummy's Climatology Corner

Professor Rummy is a renowned self-appointed expert on everything. His main interests include the climate and global warming. He searches for useful inventions and scientific techniques and presents them for us in this special section.

How you can tell which vehicles are powered by BioDiesel chicken fat

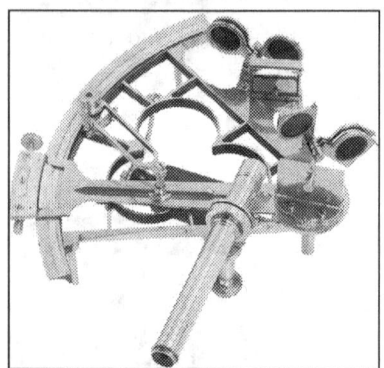

News flash: Italian scientists invent super accurate measuring device. Can measure the height of waves, the depth of ice, the width of trees, the distance between swimming fish and any other climate and natural items that require precise accuracy.

News flash: Japanese scientists develop technique to synthesize gasoline from cow manure

HOTBALL The New Sports Rage

Getting in shape for hotball

For the sports enthusiasts the latest rage that is sweeping the nation is a global warming inspired game called Hotball.

In many ways the game is similar to curling. In curling, a team of sweepers frantically sweep the ice to get the curling stone to move just that extra inch. But that's where the similarity ends. In Hotball a team of people spray water on a hot stone to facilitate rolling it down a large expanse of green grass called a field.

In Hotball there are two opposing teams. One team is called the Hot Brigade and the other the Cool Brigade. The Cool Brigade must try to get a large round boulder from one end of the field to the other. It is the job of the Hot Brigade to slow them down with flame throwers. But it's not what people first imagine.

The Hot Brigade consists of a team of 8 players. The captain has a flame thrower that is used to heat up a large stone ball made from solid Granite, from the Scottish Mountains of Ireland. The Cool Brigade must try to roll this stone to the other end of the field as fast as possible. The Cool Brigade players are equipped with back mounted fire extinguishers which they use to cool down the stone to a comfortable temperature so that the stone can be rolled down the field.

The other seven members of the Hot Brigade try to tackle the people trying to cool the stone down but in the process get squirted so that they lose their footing and slip. Members of the Hot Brigade are all quipped with squirt guns too.

The challenge for the Cool

Hot Brigade team captain

Brigade is to cool the stone down, to squirt down the Hot Brigade's tackle unit (similar to Rugby) and all the while making sure that the grass beneath the ball does not get so wet as to cause traction problems for their team mates, who are trying to move the 500 pound stone ball to the other end of the field.

As the game progresses, the

The two teams on the field

field becomes more and more slippery, presenting a more difficult challenge for each team.

Shown here is an exhausted member of the Cool Brigade Hotball team after beating the New Jersey Global Warmer Tyrants by a score of 100 to 78.

For further information on rules and schedules for upcoming games in your area, log on to:
WWW.GLOBWARM.COM

Europeans Draft Plan To Avoid Global Warming Flooding In Cities

By Fritz Krackers
The Hamburg Press

HAMBURG—Stories abound about the possible flooding of Europe because all the ice in Greenland is melting.

Scientists predict that if and when this happens, the entire ocean will rise by at least six feet, and possibly much more.

While this is not expected to happen for a few years anyway, researchers are not wasting any time preparing for the potential disaster.

Helium filled balloons attached to every building

Dr. Hans Litehead at the Institute for Social Research has formulated a plan to attach gigantic balloons filled with helium to all the buildings and major structures in every city in the country. When the ground becomes soft and porous as a result of the flooding, the buildings will float slightly. The balloons will lift the structures up, to avoid the flooding.

Skeptics wonder about the danger of the buildings simply floating away, however Litehead replied "we will simply chain all the structures together, and then to a big thing on the ground."

Citizens are also encouraged to attach the helium balloons to their house, garages and even cars. In fact, one researcher suggested that attaching the balloons to cars will make them lighter, and subsequently less gasoline will be required to drive them.

> ## "Floating cities are the only way. Hang the cost, we have to save the people from sinking!"

Asked about roads and travel in general, Litehead replied that much like Venice in Italy, people would quickly adapt to the idea of using boats for transportation.

Standard BusBoat with helium balloons

Numerous vehicle designs have been proposed, such as the BusBoat, pictured here, the TrainBoat, the MacTruckBoat, and even personal items such as the CarBoat and WheelbarrowBoat.

"By working together and adapting to water transportation," Litehead says, "everyone will soon be happy again."

The next big challenge will be growing plants and animals that can easily adapt to a salt-water diet.

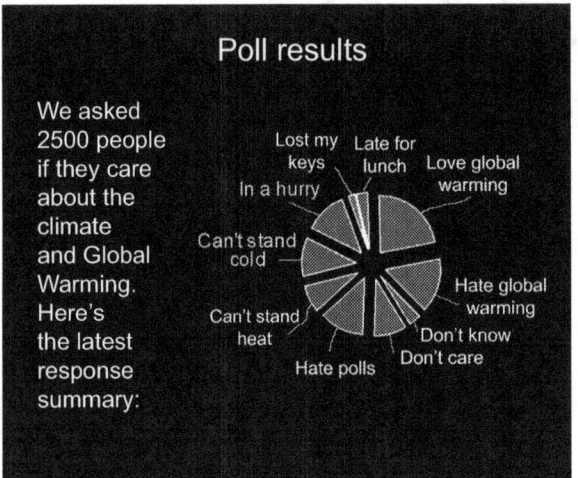

Poll results

We asked 2500 people if they care about the climate and Global Warming. Here's the latest response summary:

Lost my keys
Late for lunch
Love global warming
In a hurry
Can't stand cold
Hate global warming
Can't stand heat
Don't know
Don't care
Hate polls

"I Don't like the looks of this!"

Disaster Looms For Tanker Ships, Norwegians To The Rescue

By Olav Negard
Norsk Ukeblad

OSLO, NORWAY— The fleet of 8,000 tanker ships positioned by the United Nations throughout the world's oceans are in trouble.

Based on research from the European Climate Institute, and relying on measurements that indicate all the ice in Greenland is melting, the ECI dictated that tankers should be filled with salt and positioned in strategic locations. Each tanker is filled with tons of salt, ready to dump it back into the ocean when the melted Greenland ice dilutes the salt in all the oceans.

Barges could not be used because of the need to reposition the salt loads quickly in response to wherever the latest researcher indicates the salt water is becoming too unsalty.

It sounded like a grand plan until the tankers started to corrode from all the salt. "Those ships were not built to carry salt," said Bjorn Eglund, Chief Engineer of the Norwegian Shipping Consortium. "They are made of steel, and in some cases really cheap steel" he said. The ships were provided by various countries throughout the world, and many are

Model of new plastic and stainless steel tanker

considered unfit even for diving museums.

At the moment there is a lot of extra salt in the oceans, and although marine life would be in danger from too little salt in the oceans, it is hoped that extra salt from the rusted ships won't be too much of a problem. Scientists at the Institute point out that the fish and other things will probably just swim around the extra piles of salt.

"Salt, the cheapest chemical of them all, will save our planet!"

At the Norwegian Climate Symposium this spring, hosted at the Oslo City Center, Marianne Eglund, Assistant to the Chief Engineer rolled out a plan to resolve this potentially very expensive disaster with the ships.

Norwegian engineers have finalized specifications for a new type of tanker ship, made entirely out of plastic and stainless steel. Using this space age technology, the ship builders can make ships that are almost impervious to the highly corrosive salt. "It is estimated that each ship will cost about 50 times more to build than a regular ship," said Marianne, "but the cost is easily justified because the world is running out of the old steel kind." The Norwegians estimate they can build 8,000 ships in somewhat less that the 2,000 year original estimate at the start of the project.

Very little has been said so far by the ECI about the bits of ships littering the ocean floors, but it is generally agreed that the salt will corrode all the scrap, so the problem will solve itself.

The new ship technology, according to the Eglunds, will probably last hundreds of years. That's plenty of time because by then all the Greenland ice will probably have melted.

Norway hopes to get the ships into production before some spontaneous new research data changes all the government plans and all the studies begin again.

Oil Companies Act Against Ethanol Fuel Threat

By Rose Gasblastor
The Slippery Slope News Service

GALVESTON, TX—The oil companies are worried. In the past few years, ethanol fuel has become a threatening reality. The fuel, made from corn and far less harmful to the environment than fossil fuel, poses a serious threat to oil company profits.

With that in mind, the oil companies are rushing to the gate to make as much money as possible before ethanol takes over.

They have tried various means to do this including bad mouthing ethanol, buying out the all the corn farms they can, and telling people that such fuel will destroy their engines. But those things have not worked so far.

They have managed to convince auto makers to develop special engines at extra high cost to use the ethanol fuel, but that only helped increase the auto makers' profits.

> **"Soon the oil companies will have to admit that this new fuel is not just a load of corn."**

They then tried to convince the government that

Typical oil company propaganda sign

corn grow-ops would rise up everywhere and corn smuggling from Mexico and British Columbia would lessen people's addiction to gasoline. This, they argued, was far worse than any drug. BC-Cob, they warned, is a much superior corn that is dangerous to everyone's health.

The government, in the usual way, could not understand anything they were hearing, but were somewhat excited about the possibility of launching satellites over Mexico and British Columbia to spy on the so-called corn grow-ops.

Next they embarked on an advertising campaign telling everyone to cut back on their carbon dioxide emissions. People assumed they were being told to cut down on their breathing, and laughed off the whole campaign.

So the last straw is upon the oil companies. They have had to raise the price of gasoline and gouge as much money as possible before their golden goose is gone.

Unfortunately there are problems associated with making so much money. For one, it is difficult to store vast piles of money with all the security required to protect it. The companies have had to build huge vaults on desolate islands surrounded by expensive fences and patrolled by armies of security guards.

Special barges made of bullet proof steel have had to be built to transport all the money. An attempt was made to rent space in Fort Knox, but they were told that the Fort is full of gold, and there is little room left for cash.

Another more serious problem has to do with the actual storing of piles of cash. Since the northwest coast is the preferred storage area, with easy access to many climate-friendly islands, most money bunkers are located there. And if they are sufficiently offshore, the tax department has no chance to claim its share.

The problem is mould. The west coast is well known for its various types of mould, and paper money is very vulnerable. It wasn't long before a lot of paper cash started to rot away and completely loose its value.

Another propaganda sign in British Columbia

The companies considered converting the cash into coins, but only the Canadians have those Loonies and Toonies that are higher value large coins. In billions of dollars, the weight of Canadian coins would easily sink an island. There is talk of the Canadians coming up with larger denomination coins with holes in them so they can be carried around the neck like the ancient tribes of New Guinea, but that hasn't happened yet.

Converting the piles of wealth to gold is not an acceptable choice since there does not appear to be enough gold in the world to equal all the incoming boatloads of cash. Apparently they had never thought that having so much easy money could

evolve into such a huge set of problems.

One senior director of the Oil Cartel publicly suggested letting all the cash rot and eventually turn into fossil fuel.

He has not been heard from since.

Cooking Corner

Glob Balls. When you have finished making these treats, put a bit of icing sugar on top of each little globe and then watch as the global warming effect melts the sugar and it runs down the sides. Try a little bit of ice cream on top for an even better effect. Your whole family will enjoy these Global Warming treats.

Pour 1/2 cup warm water, about 85 to 115° F. into the bowl of a large food processor.

Sprinkle the yeast and sugar over the water and mix at low speed.

Let stand for five minutes.

Slowly mix in remaining water, eggs, vanilla and salt.

Slowly add flour a cup at a time.

Mix on high for about a minute or two.

The dough should turn into a ball and roll around the processor. If the dough does not ball up because it's too dry, add water one tablespoon at a time until it does. If your mixture is more like a batter, add flour one tablespoon at a time.

Mix in fruit.

Remove from food processor.

Place in an oiled bowl, cover with a clean kitchen towel and let rise until doubled in size, about 1-1/2 hours.

Heat about 2 inches of oil in a large skillet. Punch down dough.

Roll the dough into small balls, about 1/2 - 2 inches in diameter.

Drop dough balls into hot oil, frying until golden brown, turning as needed.

Drain on paper towels and dust with confectioner's sugar. Serve hot.

"a Tasty treat we can't wait to eat!"

Scientists Propose Huge Earth Temperature Control

By Starr Firefly
The NASA Times

HOUSTON, TX - NASA scientists are proposing that a giant heating grid can be constructed around Earth to help control the effects of global temperature change.

The mesh would be powered by numerous nuclear reactors stationed around the planet.

When the Earth's temperature rises, the easy control thermostat would be set to cooler. As we cool down, the temperature would be set to warmer.

The whole mesh would operate in much the same way as a home heating system. It can also be set to auto temperature to avoid arguments over the thermostat.

The grid would be made of titanium, the same strong metal material used to make the skin of the current shuttles and space stations.

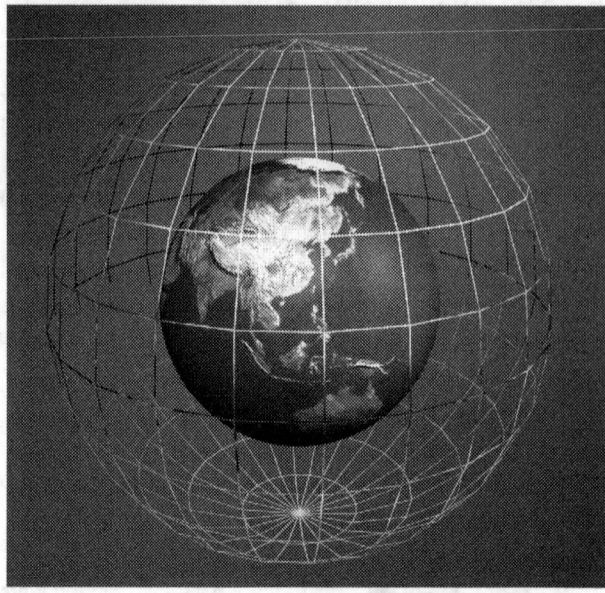
Proposed mesh around Earth

Space stations would be a thing of the past, since small apartments and houses for the astronauts could be attached to the mesh. These would also serve as tourist vacation spots for the incredibly wealthy in the future.

Geosynchronous satellites would no longer need to orbit Earth, as they could be screwed directly to the mesh, avoiding any possible danger of them returning to the planet unexpectedly. NASA scientists hail this as a great solution to a long-term problem with satellites that has been bothering engineers.

Space shuttle flights would continue to move freely through the large gaps in the mesh.

An added advantage of the style of the mesh would be the ability to rent out space for commercial billboards. NASA estimates that revenue from the advertising would help pay for the cost of construction.

Others propose adding giant movie screens to the mesh, allowing entire countries to view the latest Hollywood movies from the convenience of their own back yards. A nominal property tax would be added to every private and commercial property in each country to pay for the movies.

> ## "The great news is that this thing can warm us up or cool us down, ignoring the sun!"

Scientists are eagerly awaiting approval from congress.

If the NASA plans are approved, completion of construction is estimated to be within the next 100 years, plenty of time to react to Earth's predicted temperature change. Such a mesh is truly a win-win scenario. 🌐

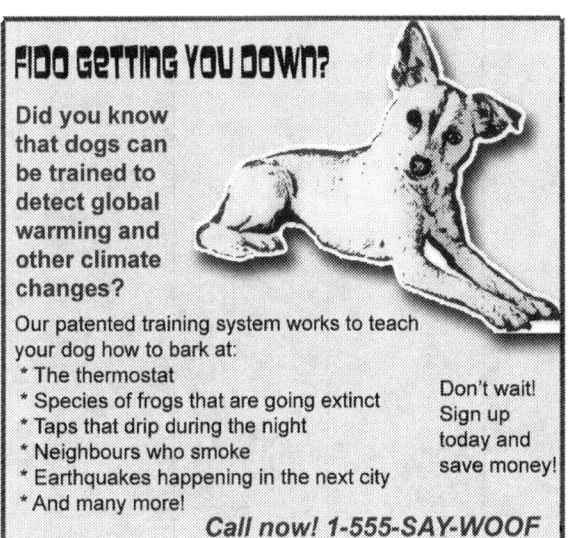
"Don't you bring that pollution and global warming crap up here, Jack!"

Researcher Builds Computer Model That Predicts Bizarre 2-for-1 Earth Split

By Freeman McYalebird
Scots Daily Tabloid

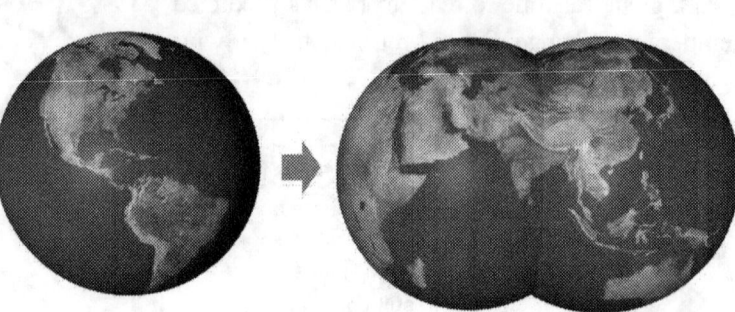

GLASGOW, SCOTLAND— Global warming may be responsible for many of your natural phenomena, but there weren't many who could predict the findings of renowned scientist Rory MacGregor, founder and co-chairman of the Royal Scots Science and Stock Market Research Center in Glasgow.

MacGregor's research started with single cells under a microscope, while at the same time he was keeping a sharp eye on his stock investment in Consolidated Hotsuits Inc. Amazingly enough, just at the very moment he observed the cell splitting in two, his shares in CHI took a two-for-one split. These facts came together in his mind, and he rushed off at full speed to put together a computer model.

But it was not just any model, mind you. MacGregor introduced numerous factors from both nature and the stock market, then lo and behold, some unbelievable results became apparent. He reasoned that if the temperature and conditions were just right (global warming had made the planet warm enough), then just as his cell had split, so too would the Earth.

This is apparently infallible science based on how every living thing in nature reproduces. "Aye," reasoned MacGregor, "if the Earth is any amount like the stock market, then my science falls directly into place." The two

sciences, according to MacGregor, are one and the same. He bases this conclusion on over 20 years as a climatologist, biologist and part-time stockbroker.

GBW 18.40 +1.02 +5.54%

There are a large number of implications to the split, not the least of which is exactly where the continents will end up. MacGregor has created a detailed model of how all the people on the continents feel about each other. Apparently, he

The Glasgow Stock Exchange

has been able to draw a line between the major warring countries, and their very continents, and has proposed a viable split. This would indeed solve a lot of ill feelings, according to his findings.

It wasn't too long before a number of MacGregor's colleagues began to question the accuracy of his predictions. For one, if the Earth were to split, there would be monstrous travel implications. NASA is barely, they said, able to send a man to the moon but every 20 years.

Having gone into seclusion, MacGregor was finally tracked down by this reporter, and asked what will become of his research. "Gae awa all of ye" was his first response. But after calming down, he started to divulge how his research has actually proved very beneficial, particularly to himself.

"Nature is very good at showing us the relationship between complex stocks and the even more complex climate."

MacGregor has filed a corporation named Global Warming Inc., or GBW on the stock exchange. The corporation seems to be doing very well.

It seems that all the shareholders in his corporation are firmly convinced that there will indeed be an Earth split, and that when this does happen, a number of new ventures will flourish. MacGregor is busily buying up stocks in such related companies as Cod Gagger Space Travel Inc., Fab Fauce Maps Inc., Frowdie Fanny's Inter-Earth Snacks, Gaishen Weight Loss Clinics, and many others.

This may well be a good example of how science and commercial enterprises can co-exist and make large quantities of money.

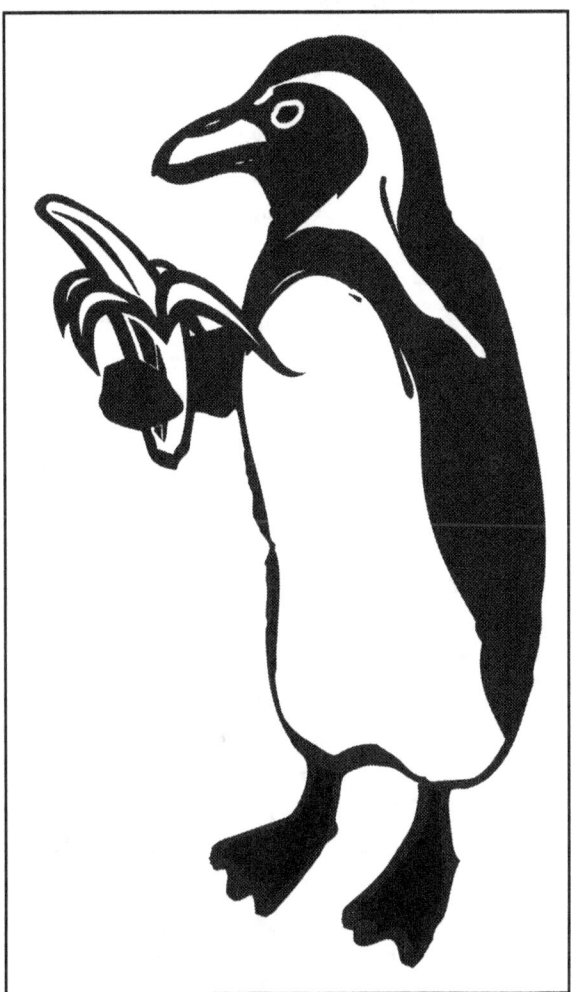

"I don't think I'll ever get used to this tropical food!"

United Nations Proposes International Cleanup Day

By Herb Hoover
The UN Blabba Times

NEW YORK, NY—Rumors are abounding here today at U.N. Headquarters about an exciting new day proposed by BeBop Paloola, Secretary General to the United Nations addressing the U.N. Council.

The new worldwide holiday would give everybody a chance to restore the entire planet to it's original clean state and life would be healthy once again.

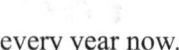

Paloola said at his opening speech that greenhouse gas and other pollutants are becoming a huge problem and he has heard that the entire planet is warming up at the rate of several degrees every year now.

"It won't be long," he said, "before none of us can breathe clean air again, and everybody will melt." There were no end of sombre faces watching at the meeting, although some members of the

council were nodding off to sleep.

Paloola continued with his description of the need for this special day. "Our planet," he said, "will benefit from our actions." "I know that in the past we have been accused of taking entirely too long to do anything, but this time we will."

Paloola's group has come up with a completely unique plan for the holiday, to be dubbed "Clean Up Your Act" day.

People all over the globe are asked on that day to hold up their vacuum cleaners, turn them on and keep them running all day. The cooperative effort of billions of vacuum cleaners will clean up all the air pollution.

The special day is planned for two days after New Year's day, to get a fresh start for the new year, and especially clean up all the vehicle pollution from people travelling to visit their families and loved ones.

In keeping with the past tradition of the U.N., a new logo has been designed for the holiday.

The new superhero "Super Sucker" will appear in newspaper advertisements and television commercials. Reminders of this type will start playing in September so that nobody forgets the new holiday.

It is still too early to know if all the nations around the world have formally agreed to and committed their vacuum cleaners to the proposed holiday project. Several nations seem to be having second thoughts about the after effects of the entire process.

China and Russia raised questions about how committed the United States is to seeing the project through. They asked that the US provide billions of dollars in assistance to help put a vacuum cleaner in every home in all the underprivileged countries.

"There are many nations" said the representative to Kenya, Oblong Angloida, "where vacuum cleaners are not part of their life style." "These are people," he continued, "who only clean their houses once a year, and their vacuum cleaners probably won't run for an entire day."

"This time the United Nations will stand up and represent the planet's cleanest interests."

Mahma Knook, spokeswoman for the United Arab Emirates, asked if the United States had developed some special type of vacuum to suck oil out of their land. This was quickly denied by the US representative who assured the members that this [the vacuum cleaner] was not an efficient way to do that.

Paloola is painfully aware of the past history of the U.N. where even picking a brand of coffee for their meetings took several years to resolve.

To avoid infighting and ensure the implementation of this important day, he has invoked a special U.N. resolution titled "Suck Up or Shut Up" and is pushing for its immediate approval.

NASA Uses Blu-Ray Technology To Solve Climate Problems

By Dirk Arbuthnott
South Pole Quarterly

McMURDO, ANTARCTICA—For a long time now there have been major worries at many scientific institutions about the global warming problem.

The problem of pollution causing the planet to warm up is having a huge effect on glaciers. The ice in them is melting in various places.

The blue ray laser in action - courtesy NASA

Thanks to some dedicated NASA scientists such as Professor M. C. Square, help is on the way. Professor Square and his group, using Sony's new patented Blu-Ray technology, have developed an updated version of the original Star Wars satellite system. This version doesn't blow up things, but rather cools them down.

Using some very clever computer software, the satellite shown scans all the glaciers looking for "hotspots" or places where the ice is melting.

Immediately on detecting any melting, the satellite turns on its blue freezing ray and turns the warm areas back into solid ice.

NASA personnel are all aglow with the tremendous success of the entire system, calling it the most successful program yet to solve the entire global warming problem.

Although Professor Square and his colleagues are receiving almost endless kudos for his brilliant system, there are a few problems, as one would expect with any new system.

For one, while the system can pinpoint a melting area with uncanny accuracy, the blue laser freezes a wider area than is actually necessary. This seems to be a bug in the software rather than a fault with the equipment, causing some unfortunate incidents.

Professor Square stated, "We are feverishly looking into the software to determine exactly where the problem lies." So far, programmers have narrowed down the elusive problem to an errant IF-THEN-ELSE clause in a subroutine of the master program.

"Minor glitches can be expected in any system with this incredible level of complexity. They'll be fixed in no time."

Observers at the North Pole Hastings Science Tent have sent a picture of one incident involving a hunter and a polar bear frozen by the blue laser.

Another cause for some minor concern is that the testing group had no real plan in place to verify that the equipment is working as designed. There were no test subjects available, which is a problem often found in many businesses.

People in cities near the South Pole such as McMurdo, Davis and Mawson have experienced more than the usual number of frozen people and vehicles. This is generally attributed to the blue ray laser, and should be corrected soon, according to NASA scientists.

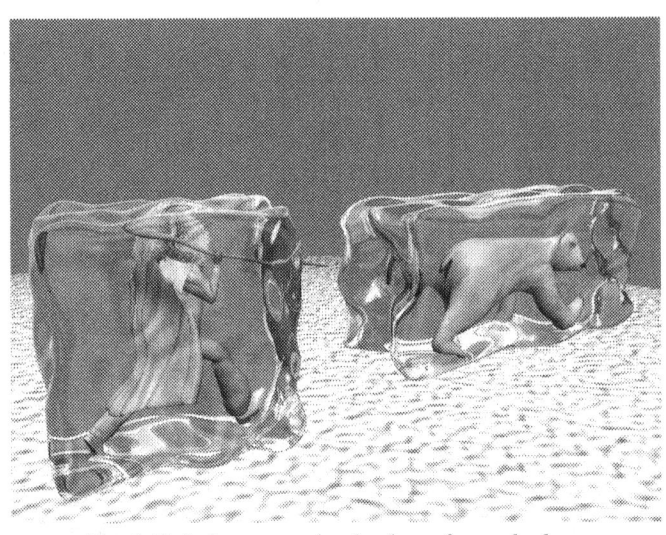

North Pole hunter and polar bear frozen by laser

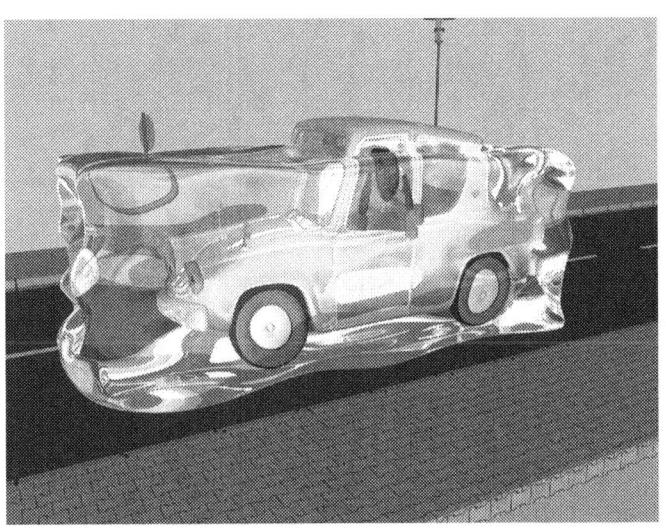

Frozen car seen in Davis City

In spite of several minor glitches, the American government has expressed much pride in the accomplishments of Professor Square and his team.

It wasn't long before senior officials in the Pentagon began to see the military applications for this new technology. Positioning the blue ray satellite over some of the more troublesome areas of the planet would enable climate control and thereby allow management of some of the more hot-headed segments of the population. Cooling down the hotter countries could soon be a reality.

The Global Warming steering committee

Global Warming Stalking Web Site a Big Hit

By Bart Simpkins
Hollywood Star Gossip Journal

HOLLYWOOD, CA—The stars are fed up with stalking web sites. Until now, there has never been such an easy way for average people to hunt them down.

As soon as a star is spotted, the stalker logs on to one of the internet stalker sites, reports the coordinates of the star and hundreds of gawkers converge on the location to virtually harass the poor individual concerned.

But enough say the stars. Now they are fighting back in a big way. G. C. Looney, chief of "Hollywood Stalker Fightback" has declared war on stalkers. Knowing how easily the general population is swayed by anything they are told, and knowing how everyone accepts global warming as a fact of life, Looney has set up his own global warming stalker web site.

Here's how it works. Anyone with a cell phone is invited to look for signs of global warming or greenhouse gas. As soon as anything is spotted, the stalker logs on to the web site and indicates where the climate aberration has been spotted. Immediately hundreds of people will rush to the specified location to see the activity for themselves. Looney or another Hollywood star, however, will get there first and hand out chocolates and other treats.

This cleverly guarantees that hordes of people will see the stars on their own terms, and let the famous folk enjoy peace and quiet at other times.

To encourage more sightings, the stars may not always turn up, but their agents usually will, and it is rumored that they will hand out "extras" contracts, so the hordes can appear as extras in coming movies. People will also receive advertisements for new movies, and can purchase movie theater tickets on the spot.

So far thousands of people have reported global warming sightings, although it is not very clear what they are reporting. But Looney's group doesn't really care so long as the attention is deflected from the original stalker sites.

Not a lot of people are buying theater tickets, but so far they have gone through about 1,950 pounds of chocolates. This, it is hoped, will also enlarge some of the people and make it that much more difficult for them to keep going to the various locations as more sightings are reported.

"This is a two-pronged effort," says Looney. "We are helping people to respect us Hollywood stars, and also become aware of the effects of global warming."

"As soon as average people learn more respect for us stars, we will all be much happier."

Asked if the problem then is that global warming makes people fat, Looney replied that he cannot be responsible for climate or waistline changes, and if people use chocolate to fight global warming, then so be it. He himself sees nothing wrong with indulging in one's favorite foods from time to time.

Other Hollywood stars are buying into this new popular web site, and are themselves frequently reporting global warming sightings to encourage more ticket sales.

"Cheer up! We can always grow a new one!"

The latest Hollywood blockbuster
Earth is warming up at an alarming rate and only one person can save us! Don't miss this edge-of-the-seat thriller! Starts Saturday at theaters near you.

Petroleum Industry Honors Its Investors

By Alf Romeo
The Gusher Gazette

IKHBAR, KUWAIT—The petroleum industry is more profitable than ever and owes much of its success to long-term heavy financial investors

In a move that analysts have anticipated for some time, the industry has formed numerous "mini" companies honoring many of its largest investors, including some who had once declared that the entire industry is responsible for global warming.

Each mini company has a fleet of oil trucks emblazoned with a logo made up especially for them. "It's our way of showing the world how proud we are of our investors," declared Humphrey Clumf, senior director of the Investor Logo Division.

"We trust the oil companies as much as they trust us!"

Several top leaders from the companies were asked why they had invested in oil, which is accused of being responsible for much of the world's pollution. Virtually the same response came from all of them - "We don't concern ourselves with micromanaging day to day operations, we are too busy running the company to be concerned with that sort of trivia."

However all those asked were thrilled with the idea of having trucks and other vehicles showing off their own personal logos. "The advertising alone," said Myrna Diptz, president of Loblaws Grocery chain, "will reap huge rewards." "I can't wait to go for a ride on of those giant trucks," said Diptz.

Typical partner oil truck with logo

"When it comes to tough decisions, the oil companies once listened to our demands."

When quizzed further about their heavy investments in oil companies, several replied that investing in oil was a sure fire way to control the industry and that they could stop people's addiction to oil anytime by shutting them [the oil companies] down.

"One day son, this whole planet will be ours!"

Rapper 1Degree Takes On Global Warming

By Nosmo King
Musician's Billboard Quarterly

MEMPHIS, TN—The battle is on against the scourge that is trying to destroy our climate. That enemy is called "Global Warming" and rapper 1Degree is confronting it face on with his new CD **BURN THE OIL MAN**.

1D has some harsh words for the Warming, as well as the causes he believes are behind it all. Those include the government, big industry and the oil barons. His attack rap "Burn so Burn" starts out like this:

I'm at the melting pole with my frozen soul
Don't gimme all your ice cause that ain't real nice
Don't gimme all your warm cause that ain't real norm
Harsh baby, harsh you make all that gas
Oil men so greedy with their big fat ass
Burn so burn

The government so slow, what's for them they wanna know
If they give their greed a miss they can't fill the air with piss
Ignore the oil men's tribe while they waiting for a bribe
Earth gets warmer while we all wait around
Then we gonna freeze when we sink into the ground
Burn so burn

And he goes on to tell us how this started and what can be done to stop it.

The CD includes a full size 24"x36" poster showing his deep feelings.

Both the poster and CD send a strong message about how we all must clean up the environment and our use of polluting chemicals.

We all welcome 1Degree and his message. His music can only be described as oh-so-fine.

Rated:

★
★
★
★
★

(5 stars)

Available at finer music stores everywhere!

MUSIC IN THE NEWS

Musical Hawkins family wins local Climate contest. Off to compete in Antarctic festival in December.

Farmer's View

Global warming, I'm just thinking
Will it stop my barn from stinking?

The time for action, it is now
Maybe I can can sell my cow

Global Warming, I'm just thinking
Will it stop my profits shrinking?

Well the government did declare
Of Global Warming be aware.

ON A SNOW COVERED MOUNTAIN

Globby says:
Protect your health.
Always wash your hands
before smoking.

RUMOURS
ALWAYS
RUMOURS

Globby says:
Wear a mask to fight
Global Warming.

OUT IN A FIELD ONE DAY

Globby says:
Kids! At the first sign of global warming, run and tell mommy and daddy.

ADVICE WORTH
A FORTUNE

Globby says:
Always wash your hands
before touching the
environment.

THE ICING ON THE CAKE

Globby says:
Call 555-9110 to report telephones not working in the event of a global warming meltdown.

DON'T BELIEVE EVERYTHING YOU HEAR

Globby says:
Wash your hands twice
after handling radioactive
nuclear materials.

SOMETHING TO SQUEAK ABOUT

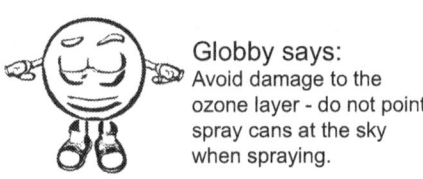

Globby says:
Avoid damage to the ozone layer - do not point spray cans at the sky when spraying.

**DEEP IN
THE WOODS**

Globby says:
Feel good about your
planet, don't let gravity
get you down.

DRUGS CAN
FIX ANYTHING

Globby says:
Protect our forest parks,
do not let animals run wild.

THE WAR BEGINS

Globby says:
To avoid eye damage
from bright xenon
headlights, close your
eyes while driving.

THE BARTENDER'S 'WARM ME UP'

Globby says:
Protect the environment,
don't discard your old
computer, give it to
someone else.

DOCTOR IT HURTS
WHEN I LAUGH

Globby says:
If you live in a polluted city go for a drive in the country often.

THE RISING PROBLEM

Globby says:
Wash all fruit in case it
has been injected with
pesticides.

IN SPACE NOBODY CAN HEAR YOU WHINE!

Globby says:
Caution: pepper spray is corrosive. Avoid getting any in your eyes.

OUT FOR A JAUNT IN THE GALAXY

Globby says:
When cooking with non-stick chemical coated pans, avoid eating.

WHEN ANIMALS EVOLVE

Globby says:
Protect the environment.
Turn off your car when
not in use.

Jason Walton

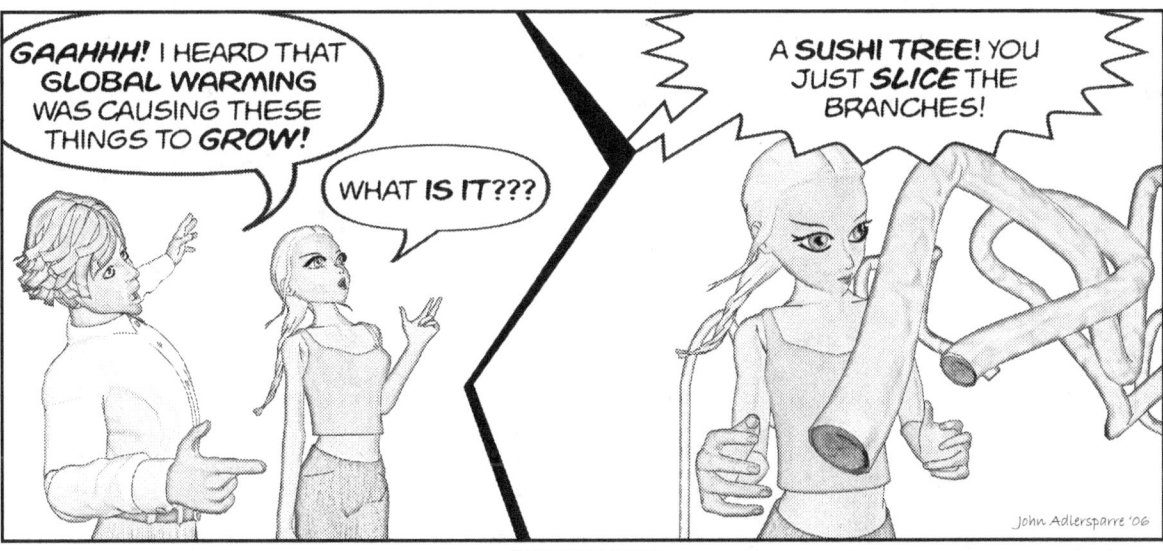

[ADVERTISEMENTS]

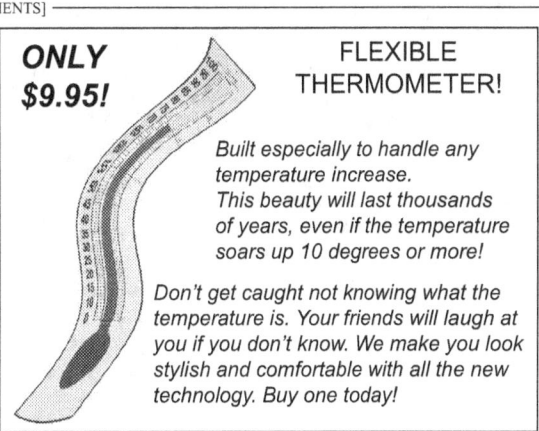

John Adlersparre

John Adlersparre

"Do you think you can find a way to reverse all the effects of Global Warming?"

"Man all these new tree species are making it hard for us to find wood for our totem poles!"

SHADOW TEXT
WHAT THEY SAID VS. WHAT THEY MEANT DEPARTMENT

WE MUST EDUCATE AVERAGE CITIZENS TO THE POINT WHERE THEY UNDERSTAND GLOBAL WARMING.

THE MORE THEY FEAR GLOBAL WARMING, THE MORE THEY WILL WANT TO SPEND ON STUDYING IT.

WE'LL USE THE MEDIA TO SCARE THEM INTO LETTING THE GOVERNMENT COUGH UP MORE RESEARCH CASH.

THE MEDIA CAN HELP INFORM PEOPLE ABOUT GLOBAL WARMING.

MORONS. LET THEM TALK AND THEN WE'LL FRY THE LOT OF THEM.

OTHERS HAVE THE RIGHT TO DENY THAT GLOBAL WARMING IS A CATASTROPHE.

IF YOU DON'T BELIEVE EVERYTHING I SAY THEN YOU'RE AN IDIOT.

MY STATEMENTS ON CLIMATE CHANGE ARE BASED ON MY EXTENSIVE EXPERIENCE.

INDUSTRY HAS A LOT MORE BUCKS TO SPEND ON OUR RESEARCH – LET'S PERSUADE THEM.

INDUSTRY WILL HAVE TO LEAD THE WAR AGAINST GLOBAL WARMING.

NOBODY EVER GOT A RESEARCH GRANT BY SAYING THERE ISN'T A PROBLEM.

WE MUST EMPHASIZE THAT CLIMATE CHANGE PROBLEMS WILL AFFECT OUR BOTTOM LINE.

SHADOW TEXT
WHAT THEY SAID VS. WHAT THEY MEANT DEPARTMENT

HOW DARE THEY CONCLUDE ANYTHING BEFORE I HAVE CASHED IN ON MY RESEARCH!

THE KYOTO AGREEMENT SEEMS TO BE OUT OF TOUCH WITH REALITY.

IF THE PAY IS GOOD, I'LL DO THAT AMBASSADOR STUFF MYSELF.

WE NEED TO SELECT PEOPLE AS AMBASSADORS TO SHAPE THE GLOBAL CLIMATE.

WE SPENT OUR LAST RESEARCH GRANT, TIME FOR A NEW ONE.

WE HAVE FORMULATED A PLAN TO COMBAT GLOBAL WARMING AND ARE READY TO PROCEED.

WE DON'T HAVE A CLUE HOW TO MEASURE IT, SO LET'S MAKE UP SOME REALLY GOOD SOUNDING THEORIES.

CLIMATE CHANGE REQUIRES COMPLEX SCIENTIFIC MEASUREMENTS TO UNDERSTAND.

I TRIED "THE SUN IS COOLING DOWN" BUT NOBODY WOULD FUND MY RESEARCH.

THE ICE IN GREENLAND IS SLOWLY MELTING AWAY.

WHAT BETTER WAY TO DO RESEARCH THAN LYING DOWN ALL DAY?

WE MUST STUDY CLOUD FORMATIONS TO UNDERSTAND GLOBAL WARMING.

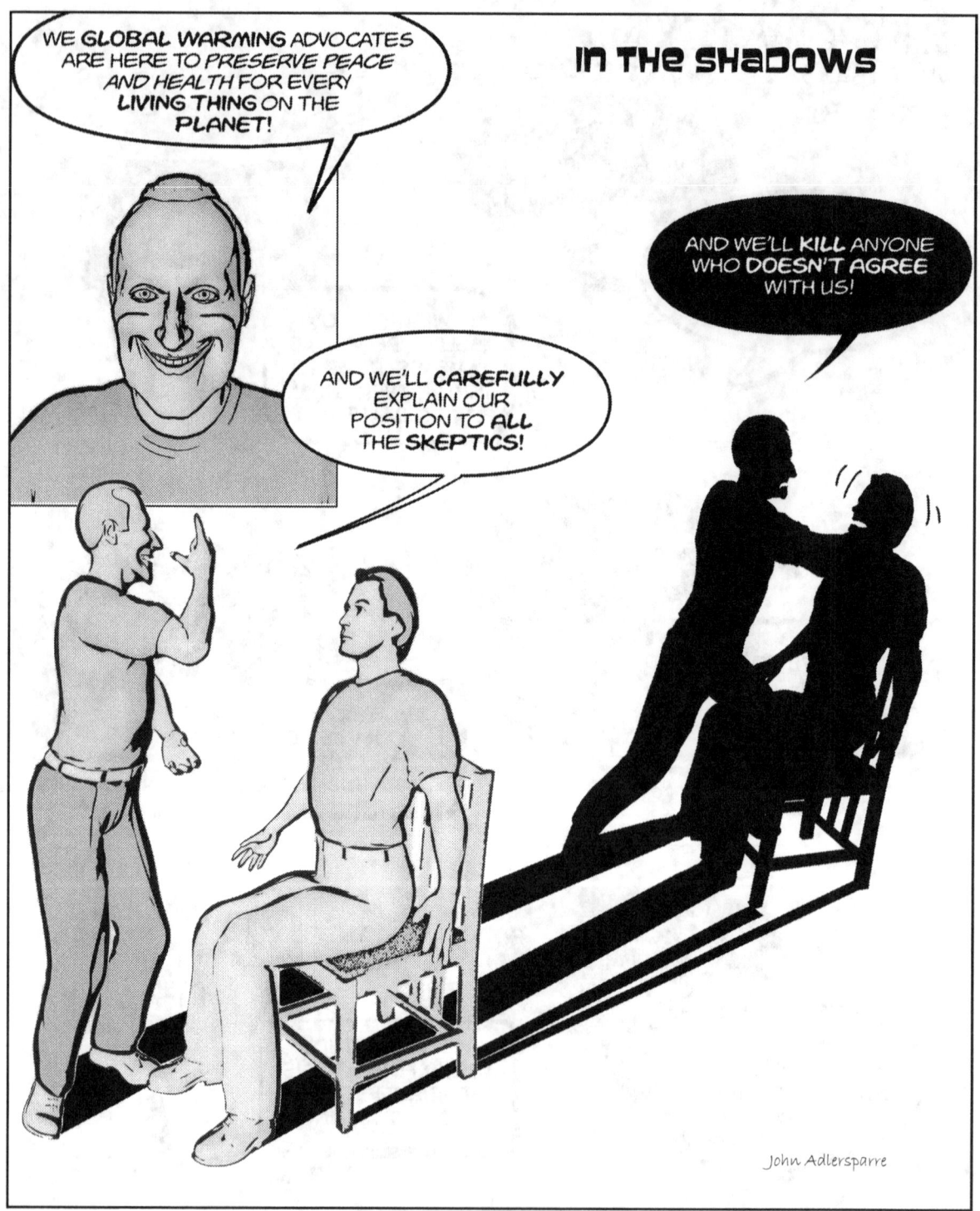

Global Warming and my Beer

I don't like Global Warming
I think it's very clear
The effect of Global Warming
Is that it warms my beer

Global Warming Cartoons

THE BEARER OF GLOBAL WARMING

THE BEARER OF GLOBAL WARMING

THE BEARER OF GLOBAL WARMING

THE BEARER OF GLOBAL WARMING

THE BEARER OF GLOBAL WARMING

THE BEARER OF GLOBAL WARMING

A day in a life of global warming

My dear warm world, I loathe for you to cool
Your heat will melt my seat

Green light pervades my space at night
The hue will never do

Abundantly the heat rolls in
Like ocean waves on top of tin

The thunderous sound how loud it seems
Its endless, endless those mad dreams

A million silver suited people with ear installed cell phones
Scurry into man made holes

The heat wave, is unfolding now
The sweat, the sweat is on my brow

The warning sirens, now are still
Oh, where's my global warming pill

Sir Gary and Lady Dorothy, a Fable

- Author John Aesoparre

O nce upon a time in a scented forest not far from the castle of King Chantelour lived Sir Gary and his bride Lady Dorothy. Sir Gary was well known all over as a gallant knight who had fought many fierce battles and eventually won the heart of Lady Dorothy at a fabulous castle ball honoring his many triumphant deeds for the King.

But all was not well in their household, because of late, Sir Gary had been musing a lot about the state of things in the land. Most notably

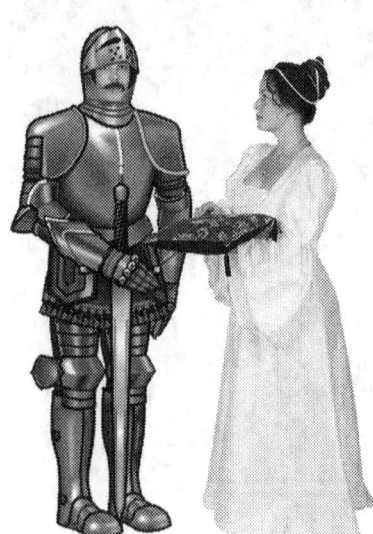

his attentions were set on the many fires and chemicals beset upon them by the new Wizard Dragobret. It was Sir Gary who had pointed out that Dragobret's constant dabbling with strange experiments had in fact caused the sky to turn grey and the land to become warmer.

Lady Dorothy was becoming all the more concerned that Sir Gary was spending most of his waking days paying far too much attention to the changing climate and its effects on all of nature in the kingdom.

In fact, Lady Dorothy had noticed that these things were affecting his every action of late.

Sir Gary would not go to battle because he feared that the noise would affect the trees. He would not have any more of his famous woodland fairs because he feared for the health of the wild animals, what with gallons of spirits flowing in the forest. He would not even consider helping Dragobret when asked by the King to help him gather wild mushrooms and other plants for experiments. Even the King was becoming concerned about Sir Gary.

As time passed, Lady Dorothy became more despondent and wished in her heart that he would somehow return to his old ways. She had noticed with great sadness that he would barely even look at her.

It was Dragobret of all people who suddenly proposed an idea to solve Sir Gary's dilemma. One evening Dragobret stood behind him while he was unsuccessfully trying to enjoy a fine meal at the King's dinner table. Suddenly, the Wizard grasped Sir Gary's chair and quickly turned it towards Lady Dorothy. He lifted Sir Gary's head and pointed it so he was looking squarely at Lady Dorothy. Moments passed, and Sir Gary gasped "what a fool I have been - all this time I have been thinking of the past and ignoring my true love!"

And with that Sir Gary became his normal self and once again served the King, the people and Lady Dorothy as a true knight indeed should.

Now the moral of this fable is that if you always look to the past, you will walk backwards into the future.

The Alligator And The Frog, a Fable

- Author John

There lived in the great forest an alligator who was feared for its great ferocity, yet at the same time was renowned for both compassion and fairness. These are the qualities, it is often said, that tell us why the alligator is still alive today.

Now one day a scientist had come to the forest in search of clues to the strange changes in nature that had occurred of late. The days were getting warmer yet the winters were getting colder. It was all very mysterious.

The scientist and his friends were trampling about the forest taking samples of water and measuring things and putting leaves and twigs into little bags.

As it would happen, the group had been walking about totally oblivious to the fact that they were treading on the carefully arranged mud that defined the entrance to the alligator's home. This made the alligator very angry since the preparation of such an entrance takes learned skill and much patience.

Having watched the group so carelessly destroy its work, the alligator could not help but come forward and let out a hissing growl of disapproval. Now this so greatly startled the scientist and his group, that he reached quickly for a long gun and pointed it squarely at the alligator.

"Aha," said the scientist, you, my friend will make a fine handbag and a pair of shoes for my wife." He was actually preparing to shoot the alligator and paused momentarily since scientists are not usually great hunters, and since he could not be sure exactly what part of the alligator to aim for.

From not far away, under a leafy branch, there was another little being observing all that was unfolding. It was a magic frog who had seen the people clumsily stomping on the alligator's home.

The magic frog, known for a quick wit and fast tongue, decided that something must be done to help the alligator. Although it feared the large creature, it too knew that the alligator had done no wrong.

Able to change its skin color in emergencies just like this, the frog changed rapidly to a dark green with yellow spots. "Most stylish," it thought, although this was not really the best time for vanity. With that, it croaked as loudly as possible, jumped quickly toward the scientist and stopped right in front of him.

"Oh my," said the scientist, "this is a yellow spotted toad and all this time I had thought them extinct. I must have this one for my collection."

The scientist knew that yellow spotted toads were indeed extinct, and yet easily fell for the deception.

And so he bent down to grasp the toad, who was really the frog in its clever disguise, and as he reached for it, the creature disappeared right before his eyes.

The scientist was shocked and his group could not believe what they had just seen. To the magic frog, this was a simple trick for as well being able to change color, it could also make itself completely transparent. Indeed handy when one is confronted by a hungry enemy.

But the trickery had served its purpose. While the scientist and his group were distracted by the magic, the alligator had made a swift retreat and had hidden itself in the safety of the forest.

The alligator would not forget this, and henceforth, to this day, alligators make it a point never to eat frogs.

Now it is true that yellow spotted toads have become extinct, and this was because of the changes made to the climate by things that people have been doing. Knowing this, the clever magic frog had tricked the people and saved the alligator.

Now the lesson to be learned from this story is that people can often be deceived by their own ignorance.

Limericks

It was ten years ago they say
Global freezing was the order of the day.
But the grants soon ran out
No more cash was about,
So global warming was the new game to play!

There once was a lady from Greece
Who delighted in wearing her fleece
But when the climate had changed,
And the temperature deranged
The fabric had melted like grease.

There once was a man from Moscow
Whose grant covered extinction, and how!
While exploring a field
He found a huge yield
Of droppings from a real cash cow.

I hear many tales from some boobs
That the Earth will melt like ice cubes.
If they're so sure of this,
And they feel they can't miss,
Why not bet all they own on those rubes?

I signed up to hear of the dearth
Global warming will bring to the earth.
Those emails each day
Are a positive way
To reduce my overweight girth.

One day an old fellow named Trest
Put his dust cloud bomb to the test.
He dropped it while sneezing,
Kaboom! But no global freezing,
And instead he is found east to west.

There is only one way it is said
To make scientists earn their bread.
Put them all in a room
With their prophecy of doom,
Then see how many walk out dead.

In a century we warm up half a degree
Seems like not much to you and me.
But if glaciers are melted
As with sun they are pelted,
From underwater it will be hard to see.

There was a wise woman from Nanoot
Whose research took her back to the root.
She found in her quest
One solution was best -
To stop the whole planet and reboot!

Interview with the Knotkahn tree people
Matt and Eleanor Knotkahn talk about their new species

After the Global Warming catastrophe a number of evolutionary changes occurred. This is the story of one new species that tells us how they adapted to the new Earth.

CBC:
Welcome Mr. and Ms. Knotkahn. It is very exciting for the audience to meet an entirely new species. Can you tell us about yourselves?

Matt:
Well after the Great Change, Eleanor and I decided to branch out, leave the forest and put down roots here in Ontario. We seeded (can I say that on television?) two beautiful children, Lief and Flora.

CBC:
How are the children getting along with others in their new environment?

Eleanor:
They seem to be fine, but we know that Lief pines for the old days and misses his best friend Sandy. They used to play a lot of board games together.

CBC:
Have you kept in contact with your relatives?

Matt:
Oh yes. We have a huge family tree. Of course, not all our relatives are clear cut citizens. There's Uncle Garry, for example. He has a terrible problem with oak wood alcohol. And aunt Hazel, a real obsession with her ash. You know, the kind of ash that drops from those naughty rolled up joints.

CBC:
So Eleanor, do you and Matt think leaving the forest was a good idea in the long run?

Eleanor:
Oh yes, definitely. In fact we have kept a log of our travels and any problems along the way. Matt has assured me that he won't be a deadwood and go against the grain with any of the new things we encounter.

CBC:
Matt, what do you do for a living?

Matt:
First it was really rough, but then my brother Douglas and I saw the need to knock together a museum devoted to our kind. He wanted to go with a horror museum, you know, buy an old sawmill and set up scary displays, but I insisted on a real down to earth museum. We bought an old barn and spruced it up.

CBC:
And Eleanor, do you work in the home?

Eleanor:
Oh no. The kids are not saplings anymore, so I have a full time job counselling new arrivals in a special program called "Treehab". It's completely funded and seems very 'poplar' with our kind.

CBC:
What would you say is the biggest challenge facing new arrivals?

Matt:
I'd say getting here. We had to reserve two seasons in advance for a place on an old run down Heisler logging train. It wasn't much fun being bundled with a pack of strangers with who knows what fungus diseases. I heard one old guy had root rot.

CBC:
Well I'd like to thank you for taking the time to talk with us. I know the audience has learned a lot about another fine bunch of people.

GLOBAL FASHION CHANGE

THE WORLD IS A PLACE OF EVOLUTION

HERE COMES OUR FUTURE

Global warming is changing the planet, and the fashion industry is not about to be left behind. Exciting new fabrics are available that are aimed squarely at the changing climate. Resistant to temperature change, the new *Fabrica Metallica* is here to make a bold new statement and make a place for itself in every designer's repertoire.

DYNAMIC COLOR CHANGING FABRIC

This magical fabric changes color by reflecting your surroundings. No need to even think about color choices. And if you really do want to emphasize a color, just wear a scarf or wrap to **reflect** your mood. Amazing!

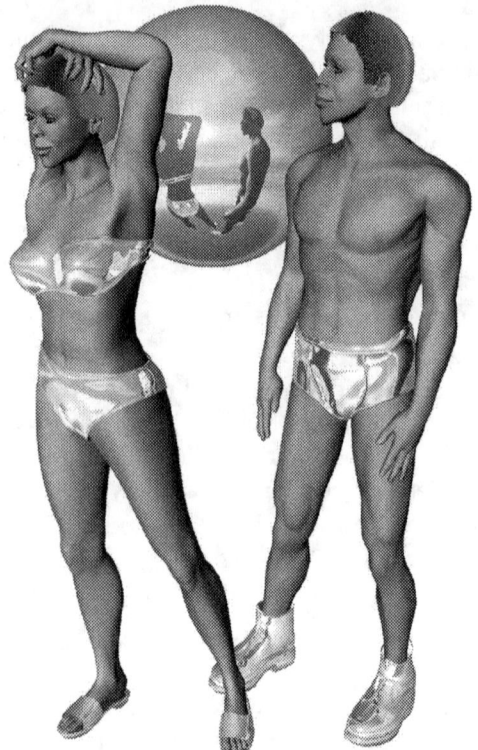

A COLOR EXPLOSION

There's absolutely no end to the color spectrum available. Perhaps the only consideration is where will you be when you wear that new flowing gown? Remember, it will reflect whatever else is in the room. It's a solid fabric, and so light that one designer is hinting at double garments, letting you remove one and have a second choice underneath. Wow!

THERE'S NO END TO THE MAGIC

The fabric can be lightly colored and reflects light and heat just like a mirror, making it indispensable in under, inner and outer garments. It's light, soft and (dare we say it?) long wearing. While it is being produced as fast as possible, the new fabric is in short supply, meaning that prices are a bit steep. But the artistic and futuristic look far outweigh any thoughts about cost. So get ready for the new spring look. We can't wait to see how Prada, Dior and Sung integrate this fabulous new material.

DOES THIS MATERIAL BREATHE?

Well yes, it certainly does, say the experts at Fabrica Metallica. In fact, it is even more healthy than good old cotton. It's made from strands of metal that are so fine you can only see individual ones with a microscope. And yes, you can swim and sunbathe in it without getting baked!

Commentary by an Old-timer

Global Warming makes everything warm.

A lot of young people don't know that, you know what I mean? I don't know what they learn in them government schools these days. It sure ain't about Global Warming, I can tell you that.

You know, I've been around. I know. My daddy didn't spare the rod and I appreciate that. My daddy always used to say: "Son..." Well I can't remember the rest, but it was good advice and it will be with me for the rest of my life.

My daddy beat it into me. That's how you learn. What you newspaper folk and scientists don't understand is that you have to live in an Igloo to fully understand Global Warming.

You have to feel the water dripping on your skin at night. Then you learn. Ice and sunshine just don't mix, you know what I mean? That's why the sun is not made out of ice. After the big bang, everything changed. Now ice caps are melting more quickly than ever before but at a slower pace.

I know that sounds confusing to you so I'll explain it too you. I never explained this to anyone before. You see Global Warming is invisible. You just can't see it. Not even on a clear day. It came to the Earth in an invisible form. That's why we don't notice it in the bigger cities. It's like a microwave oven. You can't see them microwaves right?

Well that's just the way it is.

106 Education & Trade Schools

WEB DESIGNER & Developer, Climate change, Global Warming. Spring semester 3 certification programs. 6-month optional internships, Corporate, Gov't & 1-on-1 money giveaways. Global College. www.globwarm.com
-------------------221074

Interested In Basic PARAMEDIC TRAINING? Emergency Medical Global Warming Global Cooling Responder Course April 24th-May 6th in Finland. GlobeSafe EMS For info, call 555-3223 medic.globwarm.com
-------------------221677

BARTENDING SCHOOL **DRINK TO THE CLIMATE! BARTENDING SQUIRREL FOODSAFE** 555-2315
-------------------222794

GW Trades College Global Warming Construction Starts May 15. Completing this 6 month course and on the job training can qualify you for one year of credit towards your Climate Master Carpentry Apprenticeship Info 555-8121
-------------------222874

112 Music Art & Dance Teachers

SING WELL - SPEAK WELL Vocal training   555-1465 Join the Climate Choir today! **Gift Certificates**
-------------------224171

Learn to control the climate with the Magic Flute. Play while singing the Global Warming anthem. 555-2717 Ray or John
-------------------224265

Join our winning movie team. Star in a climate horror movie.
HELL ON EARTH Over 18 only please! 555-2679 ask for Candy
-------------------226371

122 Accounting Bookkeeping

OFFICE Administrator for Phoenix based Global Warming research company. Strong accounting & research grant knowledge req'd. Fax resume: 716-555-2070 or email: money@globwarm. com
-------------------221074

FT EXP bookkeeper in Sidney Australia. Simply Accounting an asset. Fax 555-8242. Research grant expertise an asset.
-------------------223561

124 Automotive Help

AUTO UPDATERS is a new generation of mobile engine repair which is expanding to your city. We are looking for self-motivated people with a technical/sales background to capitalise this territory. Duties include engine repairs and customer service. Comprehensive on the job training provided. Must be willing to convince customers they need to change their engines for Global Warming. Hours are 8:00am -6:00pm Mon - Fri. Salary package is negotiable with a performance orientation. Fax Resume to 604-555-4499 or call 1-866-555-GRAB.
-------------------229302

BUSY automotive shop req a journeyman technician or 4th year apprentice. Must be motivated, team-player, experience in climate control is asset. Excellent wages. Drop resume in person to Big Bucks Environment Systems, corner Craig & Broad.
-------------------229763

At CAR GRANTS we specialize in getting you a grant to fix your car to keep up with climate changes. Let us get you cash then update your car. One step all the way. Gov't sponsored 100% proven record. No risk guarantee. Call 555-1719 Jimmy
-------------------229900

134 Construction Help

CONSTRUCTION Labourer req. Climate controlled windows exp an asset. Fax resume to 555-0007
-------------------221074

CONSTRUCTION SALES opportunity. Must be able to convince clients they need many changes to buildings and homes. Global Warming experience an asset. Big commissions on sales. 555-1719 m/f 9-5 - Dave
-------------------221074

140 Employment Wanted

ESL Teacher or tutor, certified, available Full Time or Part Time From May til August $15-$20/hr. Able to teach climate change courses in any language. Contact at: 204-555-6138 or askme@hotmail.com
-------------------231023

RESEARCH GRANTS I can get you up to $500,000 clear in only one month. Minimum up front cash required. You do us a favor, we return the favor. Many references, some still alive. 555-9000 ask for Tony "Grant" Soprano.
-------------------231127

Bothered by those who say Global Warming don't exist? We can convince them it does. Call for free consultation. Bus station 127 after midnight. Ask for Luigi.
-------------------232433

CHART SPECIALIST Whatever you want your research results to say, I can make a chart to say it. Specialize in Excel, Word, Photoshop etc. No research too complicated. Phd. in Math & Science. Phil 555-2335.
-------------------233780

PEOPLE global warming helpers. We provide help of every kind. Specializing in integrated management support sectors and profitability. Consultants at every level bring proven market know how, forward thinking and ISO. We push the envelope outside the box. Help you bring your sources to the table on the same page. Let us keep you in the loop while you think big and touch base offline.
PEOPLE INC. 555-3445
-------------------229209

142 General Help

WILSON ICE FACTORY Iceberg Chipper 1st class If you are energetic, smart & love ice you will fit in! We are looking for a local ice chipper person at our Northgate location. Pleasant working conditions and room to grow in the company. The successful candidate must have general knowledge of icebergs and supply a marine abstract. Some heavy lifting required. Company benefits are excellent and remuneration will be commensurate with experience. Please apply directly to: Karl Frigid, Wilson Ice Factory, 8180 Keats X Rd. Blaine, WA
-------------------224966

APPLY TODAY! The United Nations has employers looking for hardworking, reliable people like you.

Opportunities include:

•Paper shredder (3)
•Thermometer reader
•Coffee drinkers (24)
•Secret stuff hiders
•Sleeping member prodders (125)

Bring resume with references to: #820-9130 Pork St.
-------------------224332

FLEXIBLE PART TIME GH GAS is seeking motivated, mature individuals to work in our gas manufacturing facility. Flexible day and/or hourly schedule, we offer permanent P/T positions in our pollution dept. and in our carbon dioxide manufacturing dept. No exp. an asset. Enthusiasm ok. Resumes 4041 Hillside Peak, Chicago IL.
-------------------225003

CLIMATE POLICE - We look after the climate and arrest anyone who breaks the law. We set the law, and enforce it. If you like to push people around we want you! Call 1-800-555-COPS
-------------------225003

142 General Help

CLIMATOLOGIST on behalf of our client; Elixir And Gold, previously San Quentin Enterprises (2-times voted top employer in Mexico) has immediate opportunities for dynamic team players within production of climate data. Magic illusion background an asset, but not required; students welcome. Apply: 730 Casa Grande Suite 420. btwn 8:30-5.
-------------------224966

GREAT GOLF Club has the following position available. General marketing person required for weekend and holiday relief for banquet set up, schmoozing with clients to get more research grants for the club. Apply by mail to 320 Cantor Bay Road, Victoria, B.C. V8N 6C6 or by email to officeadmin@globwarm. com or by fax 555-5365. No phone calls
-------------------224903

FT/PT uniformed security required for a variety of work locations. Must be customer service oriented. Must be able to protect us against Global Warming militant advocates. 8ST1 &2 not required, but an asset. Contact Bob Goldthwaite at 555-1855. Leave message.
-------------------224871

BROWN LAKE Garden Centre requires FT seasonal retail staff. Some plant knowledge. Must know how to convince customers to buy lots of plants to clean up carbon dioxide. 1662 Hwy 15 near Long Exit.
-------------------223007

VICTORIA GLOBAL WARMING ZOO is accepting resumes for Mgr/ Asst Manager, summer tour guides & gift shop personnel. Also need staff to care for endangered species animals and plants grown and raised right here. Apply to 777 Blightey Street, Victoria.

Apply Now For Summer Jobs!
-------------------236599

Global Warming Classifieds

164 Professional & Management

INSURANCE

We are currently seeking a high energy, career-oriented individual who has experience in Global Warming and Cooling. We would welcome your application no matter what your Licensing level may be. Responsibilities can be tailored in accordance with your particular experience, abilities and your career aspirations. In addition to competitive salary and a comprehensive benefits plan. We also offer performance bonuses as well as attractive working conditions.

Send your resume to:
Frank Gonzales,
General Manager,
164 Greengrab Ave.,
Vernon, B.C. V6X3W2

------------------------220122

SOUS CHEF

Electric Zap requires experienced Sous Chef. Must be able to supervise staff, have a minimum 3 - 5 years cooking and prep experience, and be able to work evenings and weekends. Good opportunity for the right person. Benefits, good salary. Able to cook up specialized Global Warming dishes and desserts. Please apply in person between 9-11am, Monday to Friday, 4025 Souffle Ave.

------------------------227611

We are currently conducting searches for: fast talkers and smooth sales people. Join our team and help customers get bigger grants. For more details and job opportunities please go to:
ggetters.globwarm.com

------------------------227611

DO YOU SHINE working with retired research scientists? FT position, HSW. Must be avail, all shifts. Will train right person. Must like hearing boring old climate change stories. Mail resume 17 Gold, 19714

------------------------233101

187 Employment Opportunities

GlobalBeauty_____

Come and join our team!

JOB FAIR

Monday July 10, 2006
4:00PM - 7:30PM
The Harriet Millsow Hotel

We are looking for a few good people to help us develop the next generation of cosmetics to combat global warming. Scientists, researchers and test subjects are all welcome to join our exciting development team.

Apply in person with complete resume

GlobalBeauty is AA/EEO, a drug-free workplace

164 Employment Opportunities

POWERFUL MINDS WANTED

SUPER CLIMATE SOFTWARE!

Find us on the Internet!

GlobaMicro is searching for key individuals who know no limits. We make software that people buy because they are afraid of climate change. We're searching for people who can take a concept and turn it into cash. It's that simple.

Software Engineers

Experts in writing code and making it look like it's really worth buying. Documentation optional. Experience in C/C++ or any computer language anyone has heard of is an asset. MA/MS, BA/BS or no experience at all.

Program Managers

Your job is to push the engineers to their full capacity and churn out saleable software products at any cost.

Marketing and Product Managers

You are the backbone of our company. Nothing the programmers do is as important as selling the products. Your commission will depend on how fast you can make the team grind out programs, and how fast you can sell them. Base salary plus commissions can earn you up to $200,000 per year!

Database and Systems Administrators

We think we need some of these but don't really know why. If you feel you know what these people do, add that to your resume.

Human Resources Managers/Generalists

Responsible for motivating lazy software engineers, placating shareholders and documenting case studies to discredit all the competition. You are responsible for making our company rise to the top of the heap!

Attorneys

Your primary function is to defend us against the continual barrage of lawsuits we encounter when we sell our software products. We accept only the best.

164 Employment Opportunities

We're N.S.I.U

What do we do?
We investigate new life forms created by global warming changes

Why do we do it?
We want to catalog every new species as it appears with each degree of climate change.

1-800-555-NSIU

How can you help us?
We need people to wander about the planet looking for new evolving life forms. You choose your own location, from the ones that are available.

We need people to wander around in places where the most bizarre evolution is taking place - the Arctic, Antarctic, Galapagos Islands and downtown New York.

N.S.I.U. is a volunteer organization so don't expect to be paid anything. Do bring warm boots and plenty of sandwiches along with a pen and some paper.

164 Employment Opportunities

Climate Change Fair
Tuesday July 11
11:00AM - 3:00PM
GW Bush Center
1100 Fifth St.
Magnolia, DE

* Researchers
* Observers
* Engineers
* Technical Writers
* Software writers
* Office boys/girls
* Managers
* Presidents

* Politicians
* Product Designers
* Lawyers
* Movie Directors
* Architects

Anyone who can sell the idea of climate change to a naive audience!

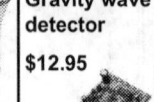

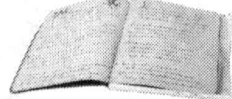

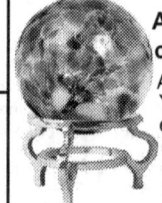

Global Warming concert getting closer - may be drifting toward Australia

New Gospel Climate hymns abound in local churches

Shortage of ice cancels Greenland Global Warming Festival

OUR MISTAKE!

Last month we reported that several global warming advocates had kidnapped a global warming skeptic and were holding her for ransom. Since no ransom note has been received, we can no longer assume it was a real kidnapping, probably just a college prank. Sorry - ed.

Research Do's and Don'ts

When you finally get your research grant to study Global Warming or Global Cooling, or whatever other disaster you have cooked up to study, remember these tips during your presentation. Always have your next research grant in mind and be careful how you present your results.

Do use logic when you make a claim. Don't say something like "pollution makes more clouds so the earth will warm up." Everyone who goes to the beach knows that when it's sunny it's warm, and when it's cloudy, it's cold.

Don't exaggerate. Using a phrase like "when the Siberian peat bogs heat up the earth will explode." That's too easy to refute. Change your thinking to a claim something like "if the earth warms up, Russian women will have to switch from scarves and heavy coats to summer dresses, resulting in all of them having to spend more on clothes." This will scare women much more than exploding peat bogs.

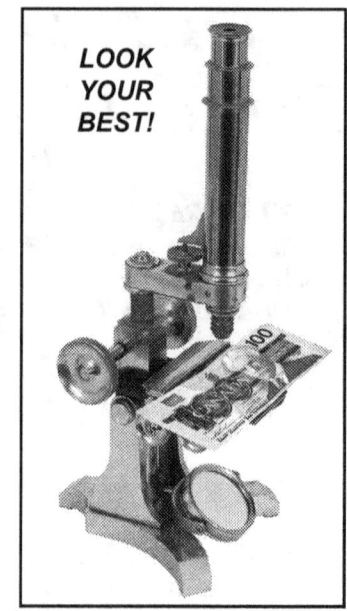

LOOK YOUR BEST!

Do invent new concepts to ensure people need more of your research work. For example, when talking about melting ice, invent a new melting scale like "crystals per angstrom", and give the units an original name, for example "CRANGS". This will mystify your audience and almost always guarantee more research.

Do use Fahrenheit, not Celsius when naming temperature changes. Using Fahrenheit is much more impressive, for example in the USA they say "boy, it must be 100 degrees out there" but in Canada they say "boy it must be 37.78 degrees out there" - see how unimpressive the Canadians are?

Don't overdo it when talking about carbon dioxide emissions. Remember people breathe out carbon dioxide, and you don't want to offend your grant givers. Be careful never to mention breathing out, just concentrate on all the breathing in problems with pollution.

Do translate all your statements to simple laymen terms so even the people who are too stupid to get research grants will understand you. For example, when talking about the ocean warming up, remember that some people will try to swim in the middle of winter assuming the ocean is now warm. Use other terms like "the ocean to air temperature ratio will differ," which is clearly better because it says nothing.

Don't use absolute terms when there are so many alternatives. For example, don't say "the ice at the polar ice caps will melt," rather than use "will" use another more vague term like "might", or "may" or "could" and so on. Drawing specific conclusions makes your research much too easy to disprove.

Do remember to draw your conclusions carefully. When you sum up your research, make sure you imply it is much too early to make any conclusions, and much more research is required. This will ensure you can easily get more grants.

Don't forget the critical importance of claiming that all your tests were done on lab animals, and much more research is required to prove the results on humans. Take a lesson from medical researchers and then you can say that your research has proven itself to succeed, now you need a much bigger grant for human tests. Few people will understand or even care what you are talking about so the field is yours.

Do take pride in the fact that people will believe everything you say, but be gentle with them. Saying that earth will melt in a few months might scare some people. Say it is a gradual process over hundreds of years, and everyone will relax since nobody lives that long anyway.

Do always keep in mind that most people have the attention span of a flash cube, so make your statements socially significant. Relating global warming to fashion and video games will be far more successful than some boring topic like extinction or climate change.

Don't ever forget the power of the obvious. No matter how many times you say "what many people fail to realize is that the warming really is global," it sounds impressive, says nothing, and rounds out your research results. There are many other useless phrases like this that you should catalog and re-use as often as possible.

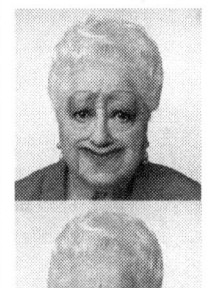

Reading a grant award manager's expression...

"Yes I will give you the grant but reluctantly!"

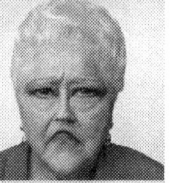

"I have to think about how to turn this one down!"

"I don't even like the way you look!"

"Get out of here and never come back!"

"There's an email spammer at the door who says he'll give us an 8 million dollar research grant if we give him our credit card and bank account number!"

WINCHESTER THE RESEARCH COMPUTER

THE SOUND
OF RESEARCH

WINCHESTER THE RESEARCH COMPUTER

ONE DAY
IN FLORIDA
AFTER
GLOBAL
COOLING BUT
BEFORE
GLOBAL
WARMING

WINCHESTER THE RESEARCH COMPUTER

GLOBAL
WARMING
ATTRACTS
ALL KINDS

WINCHESTER THE RESEARCH COMPUTER

THE PRINCESS
IN RESEARCH
FAIRYLAND

WINCHESTER THE RESEARCH COMPUTER

LOOK WHO'S
TALKING

WINCHESTER THE RESEARCH COMPUTER

SPEAKING
THE WRITE
LANGUAGE

WINCHESTER THE RESEARCH COMPUTER

INCREASED
CAPACITY

WINCHESTER THE RESEARCH COMPUTER

IT'S A CRYING SHAME!

WINCHESTER THE RESEARCH COMPUTER

THE ANNOYING
HAND-HELD COMPUTER

WINCHESTER THE RESEARCH COMPUTER

THE
BUSY
PRINTER

WINCHESTER THE RESEARCH COMPUTER

THE
NEW
PRINTER

WINCHESTER THE RESEARCH COMPUTER

THE HIDDEN
RESEARCH
DATA

WINCHESTER THE RESEARCH COMPUTER

CHANGING
MODES

AT THE PRESS OF A KEY I CAN *SWITCH* TO EARTH TEMPERATURE DATA!

OR I CAN *SWITCH* TO TIDAL WAVE DATA OR *SWITCH* TO EARTHQUAKE DATA!

NOW I KNOW WHAT THEY MEAN BY "*DIP SWITCH!*"

ADLERSPARRE '06

WINCHESTER THE RESEARCH COMPUTER

TIME TO
UPDATE
THE OLD
CHASSIS

WINCHESTER THE RESEARCH COMPUTER

DO IT
YOURSELF
THEN

WINCHESTER THE RESEARCH COMPUTER

WINCHESTER
LEARNS
A LESSON

WINCHESTER THE RESEARCH COMPUTER

SHARING
CAN BE
FUN

WINCHESTER THE RESEARCH COMPUTER

THE ART OF
RESEARCH

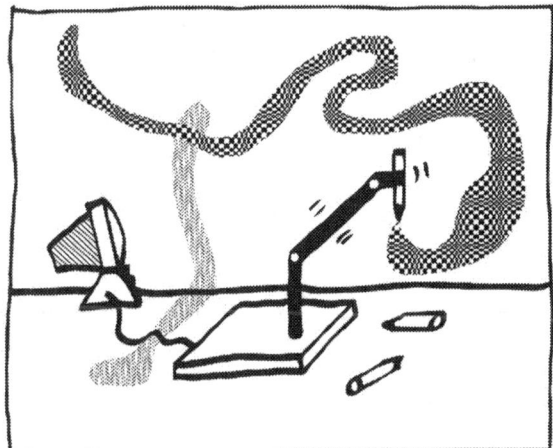

WINCHESTER THE RESEARCH COMPUTER

ONE DAY
AT THE
POLICE
STATION

WINCHESTER THE RESEARCH COMPUTER

THE
TOWER
OF
BABEL
REVISITED

WINCHESTER THE RESEARCH COMPUTER

HOUSE-
KEEPING
IS A DRAG

WINCHESTER THE RESEARCH COMPUTER

ONE
FINE
SUMMER
DAY

WINCHESTER THE RESEARCH COMPUTER

THE
RESEARCH
TRIP

WINCHESTER THE RESEARCH COMPUTER

THE
MYSTIFIED
TECHNICIAN

WINCHESTER THE RESEARCH COMPUTER

EVERYTHING
IS RELATIVE

WINCHESTER THE RESEARCH COMPUTER

SPREADING
THE WORD

WINCHESTER THE RESEARCH COMPUTER

CUTTING IT
CLOSE

www.ingramcontent.com/pod-product-compliance
Lightning Source LLC
Chambersburg PA
CBHW082326290526
45793CB00007B/781